A. K.'S FLY BOX

A. K.'S FLY BOX

A.K. Best

Foreword by John Gierach

LYONS & BURFORD, PUBLISHERS

Printed in Hong Kong

Design by MRP Design.

Composition by Ling Lu, CompuDesign

10 9 8 7 6 5 4 3 2 1

Library of Congress Cataloging-in-Publication Data

Best, A. K., 1933–
    A. K.'S fly box / A. K. Best; foreword by John Gierach.
        p.   cm.
    Includes index.
    ISBN 1–55821-362-7 (cloth)
    1. Flies, Artificial. 2. Flies, Artificial—Pictorial works. 3. Fly tying. I. Title.
SH451.B4525   1996
799. 1' 2—dc20   95–31161
                                                               CIP

To my three Angels, Suzanne, Alecia, and Elizabeth

Contents

Introduction

I have a collection of flies that, somewhere over the last few years, has begun to slop over from a big desk drawer into a cardboard box. Someday I'm going to get it organized, maybe even displayed, but so far all I've managed to do is get most of the flies in plastic boxes so they don't get crushed.

The bulk of these patterns are for trout, but some are for salmon, char, bass, pike, panfish, carp, gar, and I don't know what else. A few are by tyers you've probably heard of, but most are by guides, friends, and friendly strangers.

I've accumulated these things over the years for no other reason than that they seemed interesting or beautiful or weird or maybe even ridiculous in some strangely meaningful way, but the one thing they all have in common is that they're well tied. By that I mean they look the way the tyers wanted them to—however that happened to be—which is the only good definition of "welltied" I've ever been able to come up with.

I think it is fascinating to look at flies by different tyers, especially when the patterns are similar. A Pale Morning Dun is a Pale Morning Dun—or at least an *Ephemerella infrequens*—but every good tyer still puts his or her own stylistic mark on the pattern.

The mark A. K. Best puts on fly patterns is easier to see than it is to describe. The first thing you notice about his flies is that they're beautifully tied: neat, crisp, and elegant. His dry flies especially have a realistically delicate look—although when you fish them, you'll notice that they're surprisingly durable.

And they're also entirely recognizable, unlike some of the new patterns people are dreaming up these days. Most of A. K.'s flies are more or less traditional patterns, but with some well-thought-out variations in materials, proportions, and colors that make them noticeably better.

The changes A. K. makes in existing patterns—and the new flies he comes up with—are based on close observation of insects, but they're also tempered by actual fishing experience. In that sense, he's not a strict imitationist. If you wonder why he agonizes over the color of the thorax on a tiny Paraleptophlebia Dun, but ignores the more obvious speckled wing on a size-14 Callibaetis, it's because, in his experience, the thorax makes a difference while the speckled wing doesn't. It's as simple as that.

He also tends to shy away from things like extended bodies, shaped wings, sculptured legs, eyeballs, and anything else that makes a fly difficult to tie. He'll go to great lengths to create a fly that works, but he also has the strong practical streak of the longtime professional tyer. One thing A. K. won't do is try to sell you on a complicated pattern when a standard fly will work just as well.

On the other hand, if an insect has a longer tail, trimmer body, taller wings, or longer legs than most, or if the actual bug sits differently on the water than its standard imitation, then that's how he'll tie the pattern. Never mind the supposedly proper proportions. I mean, how can they be proper if they're wrong?

And then of course there's color. A. K. *is* a strict colorist, probably more fanatical about it than any other tyer I've met or read about. He was the first tyer I ever knew who blended his dubbing a few shades lighter so it would be the right color after it got wet or doped with fly flotant, and his Pale Morning Duns, Blue-winged Olives, Green Drakes, and such are tied in specific colors for the different streams where he fishes those hatches—sometimes even for certain *stretches* of those streams.

I've heard him use ten adjectives to describe the color of a mayfly's abdomen, then dig out a photo and say, "It's like this, only this print is a little too gray-green, and you can't see the tinges of rusty brownish gingery dun in the legs. I shoulda used a slower film."

One of my favorite A. K. quotes is, "I don't really know how to tie a fly until I've cranked out a hundred dozen of them." A. K. has been a professional tyer for as long as I've known him, so I don't think he's bragging when he says that. (To me, a hundred dozen is one hell of a lot of flies, but to him it's just business as usual.) What he's alluding to is the kind of discipline you see in meditation or the martial arts, where endless repetition is used to achieve absolute familiarity with the subject.

He could say the same thing about the patterns themselves. He fishes them, reties them, fishes the new ones, and so on: Not broadly inventing new patterns for every hatch, but carefully adjusting this or that until something clicks. In a word, he's methodical. Or maybe relentless.

I do have some A. K. Best flies scattered around my vest, and I do fish them, unlike some people who hoard them as collector's items or save them as models for their own tying. He's given me a few—usually on the stream when the fishing was difficult and I started whining—but I actually bought most of them from the Frying Pan Angler in Basalt, Colorado, one of the few shops that still sells them.

I'm a fly tyer myself with some of my own ideas about patterns, so I like to tie most of the flies I use, but I also make a point of having a couple of A. K.'s to cover the hatches I expect because . . . well, because sometimes mine don't work, but his do.

There, I said it.

John Gierach
Lyons, Colorado

Preface

All the fly patterns in this book are at least six years old. That is to say, I've been fishing a few of them for at least six years. Some go as far back as twenty-five years, but the bulk are about ten to twelve years old. None are totally new. Most, in fact, are variations on standard patterns that have been around for a hundred years or more. Every pattern in this collection has been thoroughly field-tested and proven easier to tie, more durable, and seems to fool more trout than the originals.

In some cases, an original pattern has been altered merely by substituting wing material. In others, it's a matter of silhouette length or body diameter that has proven slightly more effective. With some of the dyed quill-bodied mayflies, I might be able to claim a pattern or two as my own—but that could probably be debated. I have trouble believing no one has thought of these ideas before me. They just didn't talk about it, and so few people know.

I haven't wasted your time or mine by including fly patterns with an alteration or two made just for the sake of doing it. It makes no sense to try to improve Gary LaFontaine's Caddis Pupa pattern, for example. I tried it, but I couldn't make it better. Nor am I going to tell you how to tie an Adams or a Gold-ribbed Hare's Ear Nymph. That information is available in dozens of fine fly-tying books.

I've had the opportunity to fish a lot during the past thirty years, and have been equally fortunate to fish some very good water. During the first few years, I spent a lot more time fishing than catching, and always tried to figure out why the trout would eat the natural and not my imitation. Many times it was simply because I was not a very good fly caster. So I practiced a lot. When I determined that my casting was no longer the problem, I looked for other reasons why the trout might be refusing my flies. I considered leader length, a finer tippet, a more cautious approach, and, finally, the fly.

I began to take photos of the naturals and compare them to photos of the artificials. The differences were a matter of a slight color nuance, tail length, body segmentation, body smoothness, wing height and color, and leg placement in so many instances that I began to look for materials that would improve on each of these factors. If I could discover ways to improve on these seven factors, I might improve my catching.

What follows are all of the patterns that I now fish on a regular basis—along with their materials substitutions, their pattern alterations, and their tying instructions. I hope you enjoy tying and using these flies as much as I have.

I've listed detailed tying instructions for certain fly patterns near the back of the book, recognizing that many of you already know what to do; and it keeps the pattern recipes easier to follow.

ONE

Practice with Quills

Before we get into specific patterns and tying steps. I think it's crucial that you understand a few things about tying flies with stripped and dyed rooster neck butt hackles. It'll make your tying go a lot easier, and your flies will look the way you want them to.

I try to avoid using the long hackles from the butts of domestic genetic rooster necks—products of our famous hackle farms—because, even though the individual feathers are very long and have lots of web (which makes burning off the fibers with Clorox and water go a little faster), the stems (quills) are too thin. When you consider that these birds have been bred to have long, thin hackle feathers with fine hackle quills for our dry-fly hackling pleasure, it stands to reason that we'll find same-quality feathers at the other end of the roosters' necks. By the time the Clorox-and-water solution has dissolved or burned off all the hackle fibers, the thin quill itself has been partially destroyed. Then, when you try to wind the quill around a hook shank to create a body, it cracks in hundreds of places and breaks. And don't try to use saddle hackles, because you'll be faced with the same problem. To avoid this dilemma, try to get strung domestic cream/white rooster neck hackles, strung Chinese rooster neck hackles, or cream/white capon necks. (Capons are desexed male chickens that grow to extraordinary sizes and produce capes with very long hackles, especially at the butt end of the neck.) When I use the term "very long hackles," I mean feathers from 6 to 8 inches long. These are the only feathers I have found with both the length and quill diameter needed to create the fine, carrot-shaped taper of most mayfly bodies.

If you try to use a hackle shorter than 4½ inches, you'll find that there just isn't enough diameter in the quill to make a body of even the tiniest fly, and that it's just too short to easily work with. Use one 4½- to 6-inch hackle quill for flies of size 22 and smaller; use one 5- to 6½-inch hackle quill for size 18 and 20; and save the big 7- to 8-inch hackle quills for size 16 and larger flies. Use two hackle quills on all dun patterns of size 16 and larger. Never use more than one hackle quill on any spinner pattern.

Before attempting to tie a quill-bodied fly that you'll want to keep and fish, you should first complete the following exercises so that you'll know what the different quill diameters mean to the appearance of the finished fly.

NOTE: Always keep your prepared (stripped and dyed) hackle quills damp while tying your favorite quill-bodied patterns. I soak them in water in a clear plastic drinking glass for about ten minutes before use. Then I keep them damp by placing them in small clumps on a damp, folded paper towel, or in a shallow plastic tray or lid that is at least as long as they are, periodically dipping them in the glass of water. Check out the preparation, stripping, and dyeing processes and recipes in my *Dyeing and Bleaching Natural Fly-Tying Materials* (Lyons & Burford, 1993).

1. Place a #16 dry-fly hook in the vise and attach light-colored 6/0 thread.

2. Tie in a few tailing fibers, length to equal the hook, and clip off the butts about three hook-eye lengths behind the eye.

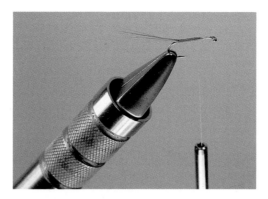

Tailing tied in and clipped

3. Select two hackle quills of the exact same diameter and length.

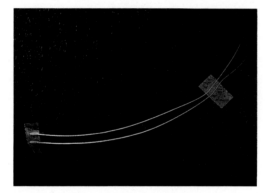

Quills of same diameter and length

4. Cut off the tips at a point where their combined diameter equals the diameter of the hook shank and tailing.

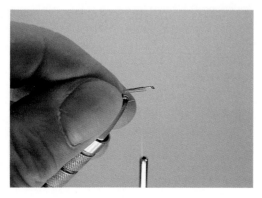

Tips clipped to diameter

5. Tie in the tips on top of the hook shank, about one-third back from the hook eye.

6. Spiral-wrap the tying thread over the quills, toward the bend, to a point that is one quill width from the last wrap of thread holding the tailing material. This is to prevent the quills from pushing the tailing material around the hook shank when you begin to wrap them forward to form the body.

Tips tied in and wrapped to bend

7. Begin wrapping the quills forward to form a mayfly body. One quill should become the leader; the other should become the follower and cover the leader. Don't let them go on side by side as if you are using only one. And be careful to not allow any gaps or spaces to appear between the quill segments.

8. Tie off the quill butts on top of the hook shank with five or six turns of thread, and clip them off as close to the thread wraps as possible. Cover the clipped butts with thread to form a very smooth platform for the wing tie-in.

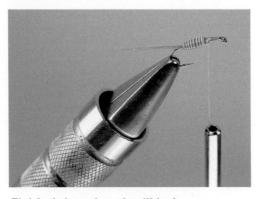

Finished cigar-shaped quill body

Notice how this combination of equal-diameter quills seems to form a body that becomes too fat too soon? I call this a "cigar-shaped" body. If you finished the fly with wings and hackle and then fished it, you'd probably catch a few fish. But, if you're interested in catching more than just a few, why not make the body present a silhouette more like the natural?

Repeat the exercise, only this time select two quills of different diameters. One should be about one-third smaller in diameter than the other. Clip the tips as described in step 4.

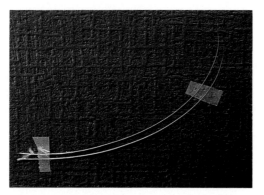

Quills of one-third and two-thirds diameter

5. Tie in the tips on top of the hook shank, one-third back from the eye of the hook, *with the thicker quill nearest you and the thinner quill on the far side of the top of the hook.* This will ensure that, as you begin to wrap the quills forward, the thinner quill becomes the leader and the thicker quill becomes the follower and covers the leader. You'll still achieve the proper segmentation width this way.

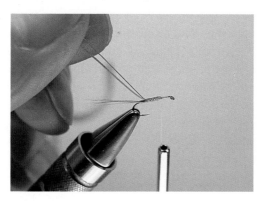

Quills tied incorrectly

6. As above.

7. As above.

8. As above.

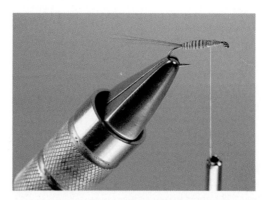

Quills wrapped forward to form carrot-shaped body

Notice the difference in the shape of the body taper? It took me nearly five years to figure out why some of my quill bodies were coming out right and some weren't! The difference in the diameter of the quills is the secret to achieving a carrot-shaped body.

I'd be willing to bet some significant money right about now that some will say, "So what's the big deal with such a tiny detail?" I have a couple of answers to that question. My first would be something like, "Well, if little details don't make much difference to the trout, then why is it that a #24 Olive Quill Dun won't catch fish when they're feeding on #26s? There's only four one-thousandths of an inch difference in the length of the hook." That's happened to a lot of us many times. My second answer would be a little longer and go something like this: "We have pretty much the same number of miles of streams in the U.S. as we did a hundred years ago, and I would guess some of them don't have any trout left in them. Those that do still have trout seem to have fewer—and a hell of a lot more trout fishers are using them. The remaining trout have seen every fly pattern commonly known to all the fisherpeople and, I'll bet, quite few that most of us will never see. Some of our more popular streams get so much pressure that you almost have to take along your own rock to stand on. I've seen fish in Colorado's Frying Pan River refuse a natural green drake! Given all this, it seems to me that we need to present flies that look a little more like the naturals. Some flies have tails longer than their entire body; some have shorter tails. Some flies have wings much larger than our standard fly-tying proportion charts say they should be; some have shorter. Some flies have legs as long as their body; some have shorter. Throw away your proportion charts and begin taking pictures of the naturals, or at least take notes on what you see when you're on the stream, and begin to tie your flies to look more like the naturals in every respect that you can. We need to build 'edges' into our flies, to get an edge on the situation, on the fish: tail length and color, wing height and color, body taper and color (or colors), body reflection, body segmentation, hackle length and color. That's ten changes—ten edges—that you can build into your fly to make it better and help you fool the fish. Leaving one out probably isn't all that important, but why would you do that?"

Now, repeat the first exercise using a #18 or #20 hook and only one quill, being certain to not allow any gaps to appear between the quill wraps on the body. Notice that only one quill is needed to achieve the proper segmentation width for this smaller hook, and that the body taper is still of the correct diameter.

Now—thinking about how thin spinner bodies are—repeat the first exercise using a #16 hook and only one quill. After the female spinner has dropped her eggs, her body is about the same diameter as the shank of the hook you're using. To achieve the proper diameter of the finished quill body, you may want to clip the tip of the hackle quill to a point where its diameter is slightly less than that of the combined tailing and hook shank.

If you practice the above exercises a few times, your fingers will get used to handling the material, your mind (if you still have one after all these years of fishing) will remember what you've learned, and, when you sit down to imitate a specific hatch, you'll have far less trouble tying the fly, especially if it's 10 P.M. and you're leaving at 6 A.M. tomorrow and you have only one or two #20 BWOs in your fly box.

TWO

Blue-winged Olives

If anyone asks me, "What's your favorite hatch?" I'd have to say, "Blue-winged Olives." Right off I should say I'm referring to the pattern, not specific species of mayfly. I like Blue-winged Olives because, where I live (Colorado), there is no closed season (except for some endangered fish such as the greenback cutthroat), and you're likely to find a hatch of little green-bodied mayflies (which can range in size from 26 to 14, depending on the stream and the time of year), as early as late February, and as late as mid-November. Granted, the early- and late-season hatches are short, often lasting only an hour or so, and sparse; and the flies are tiny, ranging in size from 22 down to 26. But they are there. The weeks between February and November offer some fantastic hatch-matching problems, because it's not uncommon to find three sizes (species) of BWOs hatching at the same time. To me, that's a fly fisherman's dream; not only don't I know which fly the fish are taking, I also don't know which phase: floating nymph, subemerger, floating emerger, dun, or spinner. Sometimes spinners of one species will be on the water with emergers and duns of another. It can be exasperating to say the least. I usually tie on a parachute pattern of the size fly I think has been on the water the most days. It doesn't always work, but it often puts me into a trout or two while I try to figure which pattern they're really feeding on. From there on it's strictly a matter of observation and trial and error.

This has all helped me develop a fly-box system. I carry Olive Quill Parachutes in sizes 26 through 16 in one box. Olive Quill Duns (same sizes) in another box, Light Olive and Rusty Quill Spinners in another, as well as a nymph box that holds nymphs, subemergers, and floating emergers. Four boxes of flies covers most of the year for me. And it works throughout the West, Midwest, and East as well. I've taken 4- to 6-pound brook trout in Labrador on a #16 Olive Quill Dun.

There are dozens of species of mayflies commonly referred to as "blue-winged olives." I don't believe you really need to know the Latin names of any of them. Just recognize that there are many different sizes, and that for the most part their bodies are all the same color—creamy green with some medium gray highlights. You'll need minor color variations in the hackle, from dark dun to a creamy light green. Tail length varies dramatically, as do wing length and wing color; the latter ranging from a dirty pale yellow to a very dark slate gray. The bulk of my Olive Quill Dun selection has bodies of a color I like to describe as "faded split-pea soup," with wings, tails, and hackles of light medium dun. It's the happy medium of colors that comes closest to most of the BWOs I find on the streams I fish most often. I do carry some much lighter patterns for the hot days of midsummer, when most flies seem to be lighter in color, and some much darker patterns for the very early and very late season hatches, when flies seem to be much darker. Once you have your rod strung and your waders and vest on, catch a natural and match its size and color to one of your artificials and you're ready. You're one step ahead of the game if you have some quill-bodied flies to choose from.

Quill-bodied flies float like corks, are very durable, and accurately represent the smooth-waxy appearance of the naturals' segmented bodies; it's also a lot easier to create a body of the right diameter and carrot shape with quills than it is with dubbing, which typically creates a bushy-looking, too-fat body. It's a simple matter to dye the stripped quills to any shade you want. You can use permanent marking pens, but I've found it difficult to get the proper color penetration with them. Dyeing the quills in Rit Dye is a lot faster in the long run, and the colors are far more permanent and consistent.

BWO natural (photo by John Gierach)

BWO natural

BWO natural

NQ spinner (Not Quite a Spinner)

Olive Quill Dun

Olive Quill Parachute

NQ Quill Spinner

Red Quill Spinner

Light Olive Quill Spinner

NOTE: See chapter 18 for detailed instructions for tying the following patterns.

OLIVE QUILL DUN

    Hook: Mustad 94840 or Tiemco 100, #24–#16. For size 18 and smaller flies I recommend either a loop eye (Tiemco 101) or a turned-up eye (Mustad 94842).

    Thread: Danville's 6/0 #61 light olive for size 18 and larger. Uni-Thread 8/0 light cahill for size 20 and smaller.

    Tail: Very stiff medium dun spade hackle fibers: six to ten for size 16 and larger; four to six for smaller flies.

    Body: Two 7"-8" quills for size 16 and larger. One 5"-6½" quill for size 18 and 20. One 4½"-6" quill for size 22 and smaller.

Wings: One pair medium dun pullet neck hackle tips, width to equal hook-gap distance, and length to equal entire hook plus one hook-eye distance.

Hackle: One medium dun dry-fly hackle. I like to use hackles with a little web to simulate the thorax area of the natural.

OLIVE QUILL PARACHUTE

Hook: Mustad 94840 or Tiemco 100, #24-#14. For size 18 and smaller, use either a loop eye or a turned-up eye hook.

Thread: Danville's 6/0 #61 light olive for size 18 and larger. Uni-Thread 8/0 light cahill for size 20 and smaller.

Tail: Very stiff spade hackle fibers: four to six for size 20 and smaller; six to twelve for size 18 and larger.

Body: Two 7"-8" quills for size 16 and larger. One 5"-6½" quill for size 18 and 20. One 4½"-6" quill for size 22 and smaller.

Wing Post: Very dense white turkey T-base feather segment.

Hackle: One medium dun hackle feather with no web.

RED QUILL SPINNER

Hook: Mustad 94840 or Tiemco 100, size #24-#14. For size 18 and smaller, use either a loop eye or a turned-up eye hook.

Thread: Danville's 6/0 #41 or #429 tan. For size 20 and smaller use Uni-Thread 8/0 light cahill.

Tail: Small clump of ginger or light brown very stiff spade hackle fibers. Use fewer than for the Dun.

Body: One light brown or dark brown ginger quill.

Wings: Pair of white hen hackle tips, tied in horizontally.

Thorax: Dubbing to match quill color. Figure-eight dubbing around the wings to simulate the thorax and hold the wings in position.

You will occasionally come on a hatch of BWOs where the returning spinners have light olive bodies. I don't know for certain that these spinners are really what we commonly refer to as baetis or blue-winged olives, but I have seen this color phase on the water—and trout preferred the light olive version to the common rusty-bodied spinner. This usually happens in the fall, when a variety of small mayflies may be hatching at the same time. You would be well advised always to carry a few Light Olive Quill Spinners with your Rusty or Red Quill Spinners.

LIGHT OLIVE QUILL SPINNER

Hook: Mustad 94840 or Tiemco 100, #22-#16. For size 18 and smaller, use either loop eye or turned-up eye hooks.

Thread: Danville's 6/0 #61 light olive for size 18 and larger. Uni-Thread 8/0 light cahill for size 20 and smaller.

Tail: Small clump of cream/white very stiff spade hackle fibers.

Body: One stripped and light olive dyed quill.

Wings: Pair of white hen hackle tips.

Thorax: Dubbing to match quill color. Figure-eight dubbing around the wings to simulate the thorax and hold the wings in position.

NQ QUILL SPINNER

Hook: Mustad 94840 or Tiemco 100, #22-#16. For size 18 and smaller, use either loop eye or turned-up eye hooks.

Thread: Same as Red Quill Spinner.

Tail: Same as Red Quill Spinner.

Body: Same as Red Quill Spinner.

Wings: White hen hackle tips, upright and divided.

Hackle: Dark ginger

THREE

Light Cahills

Before I knew much about mayflies I thought that any creamy-colored mayfly was a light cahill, and that they could come in any size. I still don't know as much about mayflies as I probably should. In today's politically correct language you could probably call me entomologically challenged. I have learned that the insect known as the eastern light cahill doesn't seem to exist here in the West, even though most of the fly shops keeps a good stock of Light Cahills and sell a lot of them. The Light Cahill isn't a perfect match for the common pale morning dun hatch that inhabits nearly every stream in the West, but it will catch a few fish. I think a lot of folks glance at the natural and notice that it's a creamy-bodied fly with ginger legs and tail and light-colored wings. They look in their fly box, and the first fly they see that comes close is the Light Cahill; so they tie it on their leader, fish awhile, and catch a fish or two. Who hasn't caught a trout on a Light Cahill? It's a pattern most of us fish with confidence, and therefore we seem to fish better. I'll bet there are few fly fishermen who don't have at least a half-dozen Light Cahills in their fly box all the time.

The trouble with standard Cahill patterns is that they all have dubbed bodies, which makes them too fat and fuzzy. The natural has a rather slender body that is very waxy looking and reflects a lot of light from each body segment. I think light natural mallard flank more accurately simulates the wing color of the natural than does wood duck flank, but I don't like duck flank of any kind for dry-fly wings because it is so difficult to present an accurate wing profile. The fine barred markings of both wood duck and mallard flank do look nice, and in many cases accurately match the markings on the wings of the natural insect. However, except for size 18 and 20 flies, duck flank wings are seldom more than a third the width of the natural's wing. I think it's more important to present an accurate wing silhouette that incorporates a functional air foil—important when a delicate presentation is mandatory—than it is to have the barred effect of duck flank. That's why I use dyed hen hackle tips for wings on as many of my mayfly imitations as I can. It's a trade-off.

Collect some sample bugs or get some photos of western mayflies which are often similar in color to eastern light cahills, and you'll see a tremendous variety of slight color variations in both the wings and bodies of these insects. Some have only a hint of light olive in their pale yellow bodies, while others are more light green than they are pale yellow. The same is true of the wings, which can vary from creamy yeiiow to pale yellow with tinges of gray or even light olive. These hatches usually come off when the streams are quite clear, and most of the trout have either been caught and released or pricked on missed strikes. This is when I believe that it's very important to build everything possible into a fly that imitates the natural's coloration and silhouette. Proper tail length, dyed quill body, and accurate wing color and length will all help you fool wary trout.

Light cahill dun (photo by Ted Fauceglia)

Light Cahill Dun

Light Cahill Quill Parachute

Light cahill natural spinner (photo by Ted Fauceglia)

Light Cahill Quill Spinner

NOTE: See chapter 18 for detailed tying instructions for quill-bodied flies.

LIGHT CAHILL QUILL DUN

     Hook: Mustad 94840 or Tiemco 100, #18, #16, #14.

  Thread: Danville's 6/0 #8 yellow.

      Tail: Light ginger spade hackle fibers, length to equal entire hook.

    Body: Two stripped and pale yellow dyed rooster hackle quills (one for size 18).

  Wings: Pair of dark cream dyed hen hackle tips. (First dye to very pale yellow, then overdye with weak tan or gray to match the natural.)

 Hackle: Light ginger.

LIGHT CAHILL QUILL PARACHUTE

Hook:	Same as Dun.
Thread:	Same as Dun.
Tail:	Same as Dun.
Wing Post:	White turkey T-base feather segment.
Body:	Same as Dun.
Hackle:	Same as Dun

LIGHT CAHILL QUILL SPINNER

Hook:	Same as Dun.
Thread:	Same as Dun.
Tail:	Same as Dun.
Body:	One pale yellow rooster hackle quill.
Wings:	Pair of white hen hackle tips, tied spent.
Thorax:	Fine, pale yellow dry-fly dubbing, color to match quill.

NOTE: If you want to hackle this spinner, use one very light ginger hackle. See chapter 18 for tying instructions.

FOUR

Callibaetis

Even thought it's usually a rather dull gray color, the callibaetis is one of the prettiest of all mayflies. I like the way its wings are prominently speckled with black, and I'm also just so damn glad to see it after days of fishing tiny Tricos. The callibaetis hatch usually begins to come off after the tricos have been on the water for any number of days. If you're not aware of this, you could go on casting to rising trout with a little size-20 Trico Spinner and never notice the larger insect. That's when you look around to see if anyone's been watching.

Callibaetis normally like lakes (especially if there is a little current from the inflow and outflow of a stream), and slow-moving rivers and streams. Look for them on beaver ponds as well. I have found callibaetis on the water as early as late July and as late as the third week in October. They often begin to appear in midafternoon, but I have seen them as early as midmorning. If it's an afternoon hatch, they seem to go off in only a couple of hours. As usual, Mother Nature determines when the hatch begins and how long it lasts. Callibaetis are usually a size 16 or 14, but many times I wished I had tied some on a #15 hook. I smile when I pick up a book and the author says, "The *Parageniabaetisclepto* hatch begins on June 11." Anyone who knows that much about it ought to be able to add, "at 9:38 A.M." What the author is saying is that he was fishing on June 11 and noticed the hatch. He should at least use the term "usually," because I've met a lot of people who will read the date "June 11," write it down, and go fishing on that day fully expecting to see the hatch.

The wisest thing you can do if you want to catch a particular hatch is pay attention to the weather, beginning with the fall of the year before you plan to take your trip. What kind of fall was it? Short, cold, early frost, rainy, snowy? How was the winter? Lots of snow, bitter cold, mild, not much snow? How about spring? Early, late, no rain, lots of rain, water temperatures, air temperatures, water levels? All this will have a definite impact on when the bugs begin to hatch. It could even help determine how many nymphs survived the winter, which will of course affect the number of bugs that hatch when the time comes. Finally, before setting out to catch any hatch, call the local fly shop about a week before you think the hatch could begin and get the owner's opinion. It's not a perfect system, but it will lessen your chances of missing your favorite hatch.

You can also use the information from your observations to clear out your favorite stretch of local water. My favorite stretch of Hunt Creek in Montmorency County, Michigan, was getting more crowded every year. One year we had little rainfall, the streams in the entire state were dangerously low, and, to top it off, we had an early fall and a bitterly cold, long winter. I told a few of my fishing friends that the Hunt had probably suffered a severe winterkill, and that I was going to look for a new stream. The word spread fast that the Hunt was probably only a fond memory after such a hard winter, and that anyone who wanted to catch trout should look around for new waters. It was great. I had that stretch of the Hunt to myself the entire following summer! There were fewer fish than normal, and I was careful to fish different portions of the two-mile stretch each time I went. But I had the solitude I longed for and caught some trout on every trip. I also saw more deer and partridge than I'd seen before; I even saw a bobcat chase a "pat" up a small cedar tree. What more could a person ask for? The moral: Gather your own information, and believe little of what you hear from others.

You could fish the callibaetis hatch effectively with an Adams of the appropriate size; it's a close match. The standard Blue Quill works just as well as the Adams. But if you're like me and you want to gain an extra edge, you'll take another look at the callibaetis and try to figure a way to tie a fly that looks more like the natural than either the Adams or the Blue Quill.

The natural's thorax is massive compared to the diameter of its abdomen; its wings are longer than its entire body (not including its tails, which are longer than standard proportion charts say they should be); and its body is prominently segmented and shiny. I've tried a lot of different ideas for this fly, always keeping in mind that it should be easy to tie. The temptation is to imitate everything, including the antennae, but that's probably a sign of having gone completely over the edge.

Callibaetis natural dun

Callibaetis Quill Dun

Callibaetis Quill Parachute

Callibaetis natural spinner

Callibaetis Quill Spinner

NOTE: See chapter 18 for detailed tying instructions for quill-bodied flies.

CALLIBAETIS QUILL DUN

    Hook: Mustad 94840 or Tiemco 100, #16-#14.

    Thread: Danville's 6/0 #31 gray.

    Tail: Light medium dun spade hackle fibers, length to equal entire hook.

    Body: Two 7"-8" light medium dun hackle quills.

    Wings: Pair of light medium dun hen hackle tips, length to equal entire hook plus 1 hook-eye distance.

    Hackle: One light but well-marked grizzly hackle, with enough web to simulate the thorax. Be careful to not overhackle this fly; six or seven wraps are plenty.

CALLIBAETIS QUILL PARACHUTE

    Hook: Same as Dun.

    Thread: Same as Dun.

    Tail: Same as Dun.

    Wing Post: $^3/_8$" segment of white turkey T-base feather.

    Body: Same as Dun.

    Hackle: Same as Dun, but no web!

CALLIBAETIS QUILL SPINNER

Hook: Same as Dun.

Thread: Same as Dun.

Tail: Same as Dun, but two hook-eye lengths longer than entire hook.

Body: One 7"-8" medium dun hackle quill.

Wings: Select one light but well-marked grizzly spade hackle at least 2 sizes larger than the hook— e.g., a #12 hackle for a #16 hook. Note: See chapter 18 for instructions for creating spinner wings with wound hackle.

Thorax: Very fine light medium dun dubbing, color to match quill.

FIVE

Green Drakes

Two of the most magical words in fly fishing must be *green drakes*. If not green drakes, they must be *split cane*. Without one the other is less meaningful. With just the mention of green drakes, you'll see your friends' eyes cloud over as they remember their own experiences with this wonderful hatch, or try to picture it from a book or article they may have read. And you can bet the next half hour or more will be given over to stories about "the hatch we caught in '67." If you're in a bar when someone mentions green drakes, you'd be wise to give your car keys to the bartender and call a cab, because you'll be there hours longer than you intended and in no shape to drive home after the last green drake hatch has been thoroughly fished at least twice. It can be glorious fishing—bar fishing, that is, which is often far more successful than stream fishing.

I call it the "banker's hours hatch," because it begins sometime in midmorning and comes and goes in waves until sometime after midafternoon. At least that's been my experience with western green drakes, which range from Colorado to Idaho. Nearly every stream along the entire eastern and western drainages of the Rockies will have green drakes in varying numbers at some point beginning in late spring and early summer. I've seen them on streams no wider than my living room, and I live in a townhouse. The hatch can last for weeks on some streams. Colorado's Frying Pan River, for example, has a green drake hatch that often begins about the third week of July, and can last into the first or second week of September. It brings up all the fish in the river, and brings out all the fishermen in the state and some other states as well. On weekends, you should probably bring your own rock to stand on. Many believe devoutly that all the big fish are in the upper four miles of catch-and-release water. Fine with me. I like to fish the water below, where there are just as many big fish, and where I'm beginning to believe they're a little wilder as well, simply because they haven't been hooked as many times as those in the upper stretch.

One of the nicest aspects of the green drake hatch is that it occurs at the same time of year that the pale morning duns and some blue-winged olives are hatching, with a few caddis thrown in here and there. Some streams have a wonderful brown drake hatch as an extra added attraction for the evening fishing. I like to do the whole day—sunup to sundown—not even taking time to eat the sandwich dehydrating in the back of my vest. My attitude is, "By God I came here to fish, and as long as there's a hatch and rising fish I'm gonna stay with it!" I used to be able to fish like that for eight to ten days straight before Mother Nature would knock me down for about twenty straight hours. Nowadays I can fish hard for only one or two days at a time. I like to think that age has nothing to do with this. I "choose" to fish hard for one or two days at a time only because I have a strong need to mediate every second or third morning—until about noon.

See what just thinking about green drakes does to me?

There are quite a number of different Green Drake patterns considering that we think it's a single-species hatch. That's true on some streams. The fabled green drake found on Henry's Fork of the Snake River in Idaho is a big, size-10 or -12 green mayfly with dark gray wings, yellow markings on its legs and yellow segmentation markings on its abdomen, and tails that are alternately banded dark dun and cream; the tails look too short considering the meaty proportions of the rest of the insect. There's the standard pattern with feather wing, yellow-dyed grizzly hackle, green-dubbed body, yellow floss rib, and black moose hair tail, although yellow floss disappears when it gets wet and the black tail isn't accurate. There's also the extended-body pattern, tied with green-dyed deer hair that extends beyond the bend of the hook to keep the hook weight to a minimum, present a more accurate body profile, and enhance flotation. It's a good pattern, but in my experience extended-body flies don't hold up nearly as well as they should considering how long it takes to tie one. Then there's the popular Paradrake, the Haystack, and the Comparadun. They all work, but when the trout are really on the feed during this hatch you can get them on a size-12 Adams! So much for accurate imitations you might observe, but as the hatch moves into days and weeks of catching and releasing it's not uncommon to see trout refuse the natural. Carry all the Green Drake patterns you can afford to buy or tie. Substitute materials whenever you can and combine various styles into the fly, but always strive to maintain a natural silhouette and size. It is also extremely important to observe how the natural sits on the water. Some appear to be struggling to fly away; others sit heavily on the water then suddenly burst into flight.

If you fish an Idaho Green Drake pattern on the Frying Pan, you will probably catch only a few fish, because the two insects are dramatically different in proportion and color. People say it's the same species, but I don't believe it. The Frying Pan green drake has three distinct color phases as a completely hatched surface-floating dun. One phase is more the color of a march brown, the second has a creamy light olive body with medium dun wings and greenish legs, and the third has a very dark dun body with hints of olive and very dark dun wings and legs. None contains even a hint of yellow, and the wings of the Frying Pan green drake are as long as the entire body plus half the tail! A stream entomologist told me that the Frying Pan green drake emerges from its nymphal shuck at the stream bottom, rockets to the surface as a very light colored insect, then begins to darken quickly as soon as it is exposed to the air. That makes a lot of sense to me, because I have stood on the same rock and taken pictures of each color phase within fifteen minutes. I have observed only one color phase of the Henry's Fork green drake—which is much greener than those on the Pan.

It's fine to know what will be hatching, but it's crucial to know how a stream may affect an insect's color. The Frying Pan flows through a red rock canyon, and there is likely a good deal of iron in those sandstone canyon walls. The result is that many of the aquatic insects on the Pan have a tinge of orange. Good to know.

There is a smaller green drake known as the *Ephemerella flavilinea*, or flav. Don't confuse it with its larger relative, *Ephemerella grandis*. The flav is at least one hook size smaller, but it's the same color on most streams. Some people think the smaller drake will grow to become the larger! Flavs usually begin to hatch after the larger drakes have been hatching for some days or weeks, and the trout eat them just as readily when they become more plentiful. Before you step into the stream and begin flailing the water, you'd be wise to watch the feeding activity for a few minutes to determine if the trout are feeding on the large drakes, pale morning duns, blue-winged olives, or smaller flavs. All could be on the water at the same time.

I've developed some Green Drake patterns over the years that have consistently fooled hundreds of fish. They're easy to tie, very durable, and float heavily on the water, much as the naturals do. I'll also include a pattern developed by Roy C. Palm, an outstanding fly tyer who owns and operates the Frying Pan Angler in Basalt, Colorado.

Frying Pan green drake dun, light

Frying Pan green drake dun, medium

Frying Pan green drake dun, dark

Frying Pan Green Drake Dun, dubbed, light

Frying Pan Green Drake Dun, dubbed, dark

Frying Pan Biot Green Drake Dun, light

Frying Pan Biot Green Drake Dun, dark

Roy's Frying Pan Biot Green Drake Dun, hair wing

Frying Pan Biot Green Drake Parachute

Henry's Fork green drake dun, natural

Henry's Fork Green Drake Dun, dubbed   *Henry's Fork Green Drake Parachute*

NOTE: See chapter 18 for detailed tying instructions for the following patterns.

FRYING PAN GREEN DRAKE DUN, DUBBED BODY

Hook: Mustad 94831 or Tiemco 5262, #12. These are long-shank hooks. I prefer the Mustad because the shank is slightly longer and the wire is finer. Use a standard #12 dry-fly hook for the Flavilinea.

Thread: Danville's monocord #62 green.

Tail: Clump of elk hip hair (see the tying instructions), length to equal 1½ hook-gap distance.

Rib: Uni-Floss 1X brown.

Body: *Light Phase:* Tan dubbing with hint of pale olive.

Medium Phase: Creamy olive dubbing (color of faded split-pea soup).

Dark Phase: Olive dubbing with tinges of medium dun.

NOTE: The light phase is effective on cool, damp days when it takes a little more time for the naturals to dry enough to fly away. You should have a couple just in case. Carry the medium and dark phases by the dozen!

Wings: Medium dun hen hackle tips for light and medium phases; dark dun hen hackle tips for dark phase. Length to equal the entire hook plus half the tail. You'll think the wings are far too long until you see the natural.

Hackle: One olive-dyed grizzly and one medium dun hackle. Try for at least fifteen turns of hackle. Clip the bottom of the collar even with the hook point.

FRYING PAN BIOT GREEN DRAKE DUN

Hook: As above.

Thread: As above.

Tail: Moose or elk hair.

Underbody: Double layer of hair from tailing material.

Body: One kelly green dyed wild turkey biot from wing pointer feather.

Wings: Pair of medium dun hen hackle points.

Hackle: One dun and one olive-dyed grizzly.

NOTE: Vary the biot and wing colors as in the dubbed-body light or dark versions.

ROY'S FRYING PAN BIOT GREEN DRAKE DUN, HAIR WING

Hook: Tiemco 5262, #12.

Thread: Danville's monocord #62.

Tail: Black moose or elk hip hair (see tying instructions).

Body: Wild turkey biot from wing pointer feather (see tying instructions), dyed with Rit kelly green. Dye some biots dark olive for the dark-phase pattern.

Wings: Wulff style. Whitetail deer hair from center of back, dyed with Rit navy blue. The resultant color should be dark slate with a bluish cast. The hair from the center of the back is hard and won't flare when you wrap the individual wings Wulff style. Keep the wing a little on the sparse side or your fly will become top heavy.

Hackle: One olive-dyed grizzly and one medium dun hackle. Try to get at least fifteen turns of hackle. Clip the bottom of the collar even with the hook point.

NOTE 1: Tie in the hair wing *before* you tie the biot body.

NOTE 2: On this pattern, I like to substitute hen hackle wings for the dyed deer hair. It makes a lighter-weight fly that's a little quicker to tie.

FRYING PAN BIOT GREEN DRAKE PARACHUTE

Follow the instructions for tying the parachute given in chapter 18, using all the materials listed for Roy's Biot Green Drake. Use the same type and color of dyed deer hair for the wing post.

HENRY'S FORK GREEN DRAKE DUN, DUBBED BODY

Hook:	Tiemco 5262, #12.
Thread:	Danville's monocord #62.
Tail:	Elk hip hair, length to equal hook-gap distance.
Rib:	Uni-Floss 1X brown.
Body:	Dubbing a little greener than Danville's 6/0 #60 tying thread.
Wings:	Pair of dark medium dun hen hackle tips, length to equal entire body of fly *not* including tail.
Hackle:	One grizzly hackle dyed with Rit kelly green and one grizzly hackle dyed with bright yellow. Try for at least fifteen turns of hackle. Clip the bottom of the collar even with the hook point.

HENRY'S FORK GREEN DRAKE PARACHUTE, DUBBED BODY

Follow the instructions for tying the parachute given in chapter 18. Use the same materials listed for the Henry's Fork Dun, except substitute a segment of dun-dyed turkey T-base feather for the wing post.

SIX

Hendricksons and Quill Gordons

The quill gordon hatch in the East and the hendrickson hatch in the Midwest are the most important hatches of the year to anyone in those areas who fly fishes. Green drakes, hexagenias, and march browns rank right up there, but in most areas the quill gordon and the hendrickson signify the beginning of the year. Life begins again with the first hatch. When I lived in Michigan, I dreamed of an early, warm spring, so that there would be a hendrickson hatch on the opening day of trout season in late April. That would mean life was truly good. Winters above the 45th parallel are often brutal, however, meaning there have been many opening days when life didn't seem so good. But those years in between more than made up for the ice-lined, high water, nightcrawler-infested streams that we endured when the previous winter had been particularly long and cold.

Some will shudder at my lumping both hatches into one quill-bodied pattern. Each hatch is a distinct species of mayfly, but in my experience the color of each is so close to being identical that I long ago figured I could tie the same pattern on two or three hook sizes and cover both hatches: for the quill gordon, #12 or #14, for the hendrickson, #14 or #16. It must work, because I've caught a hell of a lot of fish during both hatches on the same pattern.

The bodies of both insects are a prominently segmented gray, with hints of brown and olive. Some are more of a light tan, in which case I tie on a March Brown Biot. There will of course be regional variations in body colors due to stream chemistry and the eye of the beholder. The wings of each fly are medium dun, as are the legs and tails. I don't understand why the wings of both patterns are traditionally tied with lemon wood duck. Neither natural has wings that color. I suspect the originator of both patterns had lots of wood duck flank on hand, and no mallard flank, simply because there may have been a lot more wood ducks around and very few mallards. Mallard flank appears much more accurate in color than wood duck, although wood duck flank wings do add a touch of class. I suspect there was something about traditional materials as well. I don't use either for my own flies, however. Medium dun-dyed hen hackle tips are not only easier to tie, but they are a hell of a lot cheaper than wood duck flank; they more closely imitate the natural's wings than either mallard or wood duck.

The standard Quill Gordon pattern calls for medium dun tails and hackle, stripped peacock for the body, lemon wood duck for the wings, and cream tying thread. The standard Hendrickson pattern calls for dark to medium dun tails and hackle, medium gray dubbing for the body, lemon wood duck for the wings, and tan or gray tying thread. Not a lot of difference. You may well ask, "Why do you emphasize the importance of minor differences and tiny details when you talk about BWOs if you're willing to overlook these things on the hendricksons and quill gordons?" The answer is timing. BWOs usually hatch either before or long after spring runoff, when the water is quite clear. Quill gordons and hendricksons are often the first hatch of the year, coming off when the streams are still a little off-color and the trout simply can't get a good look at them. I am a devout believer in making fly tying and fishing as simple as possible. If I can get by with one pattern for two different hatches, I'll happily do it. On the other hand, if conditions dictate absolute attention to detail, I'll do that as well. We all do what we think we have to.

Quill Gordon dun (photo by Ted Fauceglia)

Quill Gordon spinner (photo by Ted Fauceglia)

Hendrickson dun (photo by Ted Fauceglia)

Hendrickson spinner (photo by Ted Fauceglia)

Biot Gordon/Hendrickson dun

Biot Gordon/Hendrickson Parachute

Gordon/Hendrickson Quill Spinner

NOTE: See chapter 18 for detailed tying instructions for the following patterns.

BIOT GORDON/HENDRICKSON DUN

    Hook: Mustad 94840 or Tiemco 100, #14 and #12.

  Thread: Danville's 6/0 #429 tan.

     Tail: Dark medium dun spade hackle fibers, length to equal entire hook.

   Body: Dun-dyed wild turkey biot. Wild turkey biots are much more durable than stripped peacock. Dye them to the same color as stripped peacock with Rit gray. See chapter 18 for instructions for tying with biots.

  Wings: Pair of medium dun hen hackle tips.

 Hackle: One dark medium dun hackle.

BIOT GORDON/HENDRICKSON PARACHUTE

     Hook: Mustad 94840 or Tiemco 100, #14 and #12.

   Thread: Same as Dun.

     Tail: Same as Dun.

Wing Post: White or dun-dyed turkey T-base feather segment.

   Body: Same as Dun.

 Hackle: Same as Dun.

GORDON/HENDRICKSON QUILL SPINNER

Hook: Same as Dun.

Thread: Same as Dun.

Tail: Brown spade hackle fibers, length to equal entire hook.

Body: Stripped brown rooster butt hackle stem.

Wings: Pair of white hen hackle tips.

Thorax: Fine dubbing, one shade darker than body.

Hackle: I like about three turns of dark ginger hackle on this pattern. Clip the hackle flush with the bottom of the thorax. See chapter 18 for instructions for hackling spinner patterns.

SEVEN

March Browns

Most of us think of one pattern when we think of the March Brown, the one made famous by the eastern and midwestern hatches. The Eastern March Brown is the pretty, light tan bodied fly with natural mallard flank wings and brown and grizzly hackle. If you live east of the Mississippi and don't plan to travel west to fish some spring hatches, it's the only one you need. Conversely, if you live west of the Mississippi and don't plan to travel east for their late-spring hatches, you need a smaller, darker version. The body of the Western March Brown is about two shades darker (light brown), its wings are darker, and its *brown and grizzly* hackle mix *should be* dark brown and dark grizzly. I've caught fish on the wrong fly in both areas just to see if it would work. It does, but not very well. I had the feeling I was catching the dumb trout in both instances.

Both flies have prominent segmentation markings on their abdomens, and I really like the way dyed wild turkey biots imitate this feature. I use Veniard's summer duck dye for the Eastern March Brown biots, because it seems to lend a little more of a golden hue. I use Rit tan for the Western

March Brown biots because, if I make the dye bath a little stronger, the color has a nice reddish brown cast. I switched from natural mallard flank to medium dun-dyed hen hackle tips for the wings of the Eastern version, but I think dyed mallard flank is better for the Western pattern. Dye the mallard flank with Rit tan to a color that matches the natural; I like it one or two shades darker than natural wood duck flank. The wings on both the Eastern and Western March Brown are slightly longer than the entire body of the fly.

I have never experienced what I would call a heavy hatch of these insects, but they often come when nothing else is happening, so I think it's wise always to have a few imitations in your fly box. Most of the time I find only a few march browns hatching and even fewer trout rising to them, but at those times a March Brown is the only fly they'll eat. Don't limit yourself to just size 12 and 14. I always carry some 8s and 10s which I often fish in late evening (because I can see the fly) during some of the larger drake hatches that I encounter by accident. A large March Brown is close enough to some of the large evening-hatching brown drakes that, if you've lost or forgotten your box of large flies, you can still use it to fool a few fish.

The March Brown can be your ace in the hole if you lose the last fly you have that is really working. I like it better than an Adams for prospecting, simply because the March Brown looks more like a mayfly to me.

Eastern march brown dun (Photo by Ted Fauceglia)

Eastern March Brown Biot Dun

Eastern March Brown Biot Parachute

Western march brown dun (photo by Dave Hughes)

Western March Brown Biot Dun

Western March Brown Biot Parachute

NOTE: See chapter 18 for detailed tying instructions for the biot-bodied patterns.

EASTERN MARCH BROWN BIOT DUN

Hook: Mustad 94840 or Tiemco 100, #14 and #12.

Thread: Danville's 6/0 #429 tan.

Tail: Dark ginger spade hackle fibers, length to equal entire hook.

Body: Veniard's wood duck dyed wild turkey biot.

Wings: Pair of light medium dun-dyed hen hackle tips, length to equal entire hook plus one hook-eye distance.

Hackle: One medium ginger and one light but well-marked grizzly.

WESTERN MARCH BROWN BIOT DUN

Hook: Mustad 94840 or Tiemco 100, #16 and #14.

Thread: Danville's 6/0 #429 tan.

Tail: Brown spade hackle fibers, length to equal entire hook.

Body: Rit tan dyed wild turkey biot.

Wings: Rit tan dyed mallard flank, two shades darker than natural wood duck flank.

Hackle: One brown and one dark grizzly.

MARCH BROWN BIOT PARACHUTE (EASTERN AND WESTERN)

Hook: Same as Dun.

Thread: Same as Dun.

Tail: Same as Dun.

Wing Post: Use white turkey T-base feather segment, or dun-dyed T-base feather segment, or clump of natural or dyed mallard flank.

Body: Same as Dun.

Hackle: Same as Dun. *Caution:* Use no more than five hackle turns on a parachute—three turns of ginger and two turns of grizzly.

MARCH BROWN QUILL SPINNER

I use the same pattern for the March Brown Spinner (Eastern or Western) that I use for the Gordon/Hendrickson Spinner. That's one of the nice things about getting serious about fishing spinners: A few basic patterns will cover a wide variety of hatches. If you carry rusty-colored quill-bodied spinners in sizes ranging from 12 down to 24, you will cover most of the important mayfly hatches throughout the country.

EIGHT

Melon Quills

It could be a sulphur dun, an eastern light cahill, a pale morning dun, or even a western red quill. It's a mayfly I encounter on the St. Vrain River in Colorado, and the quill-bodied pattern I designed for it seems to work across the county. At least that's the report I'm getting. Pick any creamy-bodied mayfly; the Melon Quill is a close copy. But then again, it isn't! The Melon Quill is tied with a medium dun tail, one cream and one pink stripped rooster hackle quill, dun wings, and ginger hackle. It's one of the most colorful mayflies I've ever seen. The natural apparently exists only throughout the St. Vrain drainage, yet I've talked to people who have had great success with the pattern on the famous spring creeks in Montana, as well as others who have fished it on some very famous eastern streams.

I can't remember ever seeing a photo of the natural, or reading about it, or seeing it on other streams. I'm not claiming I've discovered a new bug, but it is possible. Roy Palm, owner of the Frying Pan Angler in Basalt, Colorado, is currently working with a stream entomologist to identify a tiny mayfly that seems to exist only on the Frying Pan River. Apparently it's not catalogued anywhere, and the entomologist can hardly contain his excitement at being able to name a new insect. They are the only two people I know who care that much. To the rest of us, it's a tiny, dark dun quill-bodied mayfly that trout really like to eat. Many of us are a *little* curious, but it seems to end there.

I strongly suspect that the St. Vrain melon quill is actually a pale morning dun; several varieties of mayfly seem to get lumped into the PMD category, and I know from experience that the colors of naturals can vary widely from stream to stream. It's important to examine the local naturals carefully every time you go fishing. You may be surprised at what you find.

Melon Quill Dun

Melon Quill Parachute

NOTE: See chapter 18 for detailed tying instructions for quill-bodied flies.

MELON QUILL DUN

Hook: Mustad 94840 or Tiemco 100, #16 and #14.

Thread: Danville's 6/0 #41 beige.

Tail: Light medium dun spade hackle fibers, length to equal entire hook.

Body: One cream and one Rit pink dyed stripped rooster neck hackle quill. Choose a pink quill $^1/_3$ smaller in diameter than the cream quill. In this case, make sure the pink quill is the follower as you wrap the two quills forward to form the body. When wrapping the quills forward, be careful to maintain an even pink-cream segmentation.

Wings: Pair of dark medium dun hen hackle tips.

Hackle: Medium to dark ginger hackle.

MELON QUILL PARACHUTE

Hook:	Same as Dun.
Thread:	Same as Dun.
Tail:	Same as Dun.
Wing Post:	White turkey T-base feather segment.
Body:	Same as Dun.
Hackle:	Same as Dun.

MELON QUILL SPINNER

Use the same spinner pattern for the Melon Quill as for the Blue-winged Olive.

NINE

Pale Evening Duns

Much to my surprise, no author in my collection of fly-tying books wants to admit there is a western pale evening dun, a western equivalent to the eastern pale evening dun. But I've seen the insects, in late summer, on the South Platte, the Frying Pan, the Henry's Fork, and the St. Vrain. It's a late afternoon/evening hatch of beautifully delicate little mayflies with smoky dun tails and legs, very light creamy yellow bodies and smoky dun wings tinged with yellow. Looks just like the eastern pale evening dun to me. I don't think it's the western pale morning dun, because its hatch time isn't right, and its colors are quite different. Fortunately for the entomologically challenged, the Eastern Pale Evening Dun pattern works just fine when this hatch is on. And the trout don't seem to care that you're fishing an eastern pattern of a western bug that supposedly doesn't exist. I suspect this is another instance of stream chemistry altering what we consider an insect's normal coloration. An insect's coloration is normal wherever that particular insect exists.

It occurs to me that some fly-tying books don't list a western pale evening dun because the authors may consider it an insignificant hatch.

I've never seen many of them on any of the streams I mentioned, but they were there and the trout were eating them. The first time that happened to me, it was very significant, because I got a lot more refusal rises than takes to the Pale Morning Dun pattern I was putting over them. They didn't seem to like a Light Cahill, either. And when the spinners came down I was stumped, because the spinner was an even lighter version of the dun. Now a collection of size 16 and 18 Pale Evening Quill Duns and Spinners is a permanent part of my fly box.

One other possibility may help explain the mystery about this fly: There seem to be fluctuations in the populations of some mayflies on some streams. I have fished the Frying Pan River in Colorado a lot during the past twelve or so years, and have seen dramatic changes in the densities and durations of some mayfly hatches. There used to be a wonderful hatch of giant slate-winged red quills near the end of the green drake hatch. My friend John Gierach and I used to time our trips to the Pan to catch this hatch, because most people seemed unaware of it and pretty much deserted the stream after the green drakes began to taper off. The trout rose eagerly to those slate-winged red quills, and we enjoyed several years of fishing this hatch—but I haven't seen it for the past five years. Seven or eight years ago, there were so few pale morning duns on the Pan that we didn't bother carrying the imitation, but in the past four or five years it has become a dominant hatch, coming off about the same time of year as the green drake hatch, which seems to be declining. I have also seen very pale size 18 Blue-winged Olives disappear lately.

I think we all tend to believe that nature is permanent. If that were true, though, there wouldn't be any mayflies or trout. The planet is millions of years old, and during all that time, nature has been carefully working things out to her satisfaction. During the past hundred years or so, humans have tried to improve or even correct her work, usually with disastrous results. We tend to blame the various agencies in charge of our resources for the dramatic changes we see, but how do we know these changes wouldn't occur in spite of us? We feel we have to blame someone and we seem to understand we can't blame nature. But nature will change things with or without us, and I for one choose to abide by her rules. If that means something as simple as changing the colors and sizes of the flies I carry on the stream, I'll happily do it. I actually enjoy the changes I've seen on the Pan, because each change presents new challenges to an already challenging sport.

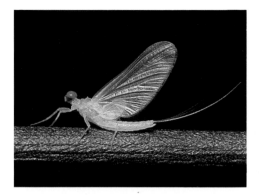

Pale evening dun (photo by Ted Fauceglia)

Pale evening dun spinner (photo by Ted Fauceglia)

Pale Evening Dun Quill

Pale Evening Dun Quill Parachute

Pale Evening Dun Quill Spinner

NOTE: See chapter 18 for detailed tying instructions for quill-bodied flies.

PALE EVENING DUN QUILL

Hook: Mustad 94849 or Tiemco 100, #18 and #16.

Thread: Danville's 6/0 #4 pale yellow.

Tail: Smoky dun spade hackle fibers, length to equal entire hook.

Body: Stripped and very pale yellow dyed rooster hackle quills.

Wings: Pale smoky dun hen hackle tips.

Hackle: Smoky dun hackle.

PALE EVENING DUN QUILL PARACHUTE

Hook: Same as Dun.

Thread: Same as Dun.

Tail: Same as Dun.

Body: Same as Dun.

Wing Post: White turkey T-base feather segment.

Hackle: Same as Dun.

PALE EVENING DUN QUILL SPINNER

Hook: Same as Dun.

Thread: Same as Dun.

Tail: White spade hackle fibers, length to equal hook plus one hook-eye distance.

Body: One cream stripped rooster hackle quill.

Wing: Pair of white hen hackle tips.

Thorax: Fine cream dubbing.

NOTE: If you wish to hackle this spinner pattern, use cream hackle. Check chapter 18 for instructions on hackling spinners.

TEN

Paraleptophlebia

Earlier I said that the blue-winged olive is my favorite hatch because the insects are on the water for most of the fly-fishing year. My favorite time and stream to fish them is September through the first week of November on Colorado's South Platte River, from Cheesman Dam downstream for more than 20 miles. If you were hoping I'd tell you a place where you were guaranteed to see 20-inch fish rising to dry flies from dawn to dusk, I just did. Pick any spot in that stretch of water at any time of day during those months, and you'll stand an excellent chance of fishing to rising trout in the 14- to 22-inch range. They'll be browns and rainbows, with a rare smaller brookie thrown in near the dam. Seeing them and catching them are two entirely different matters, however. The flies are tiny, from a large size 18 down to a tiny size 26; tippets must be fine and long (I fish a 15-foot leader with about 36 inches of 7X); and you probably shouldn't go there on a weekend unless you like crowds. You'll need nymphs, subemergers, floating emergers, duns, parachutes, and spinners, from 18s down to 26s; all should be imitative of the BWO.

That's a lot of flies, but I carry them all the time and at one point I really thought I had the South Platte wired. It was glorious fishing there for about a year or two. Beginning in September, I would arrive at the stream at sunup, look at the water as I was gearing up, and watch trout rise to emergers and duns. This usually lasted on hour or so, then the spinners would begin to come down. A morning spinner fall is just fine with me. The first time I experienced this morning hatch and spinner fall, I thought, "That's it for today." But, as I turned to leave, I noticed a slightly larger dun on the water. In a few minutes there was another hatch that lasted for another hour or two, followed by another spinner fall. I was thirsty and hungry and ready to take a rest and lunch break when I noticed yet another size of dun on the water. It was already late afternoon, but I fished the third hatch, a repeat of the first two complete with a spinner fall, which I fished until it was almost too dark to cross the stream back to the truck. I took the first bite of my lunchtime sandwich at about 10 P.M. as I was driving home.

Two years ago I got humiliated during the day's third hatch. The mayflies in the feeding lane appeared to be the size and color they should be, at least from where I was standing. I even waded into the feeding lane and netted some insects. They were the same size all right, and the color of my imitation seemed close. Evidently not close enough, though, because I couldn't catch a single trout. I netted the feeding lane again and sat down on the bank to examine two or three naturals. "Let's see, tail length? Fine. Body? A little lighter than my Olive Quill Dun. Wings? They're about right. Wait. Thorax! The natural has a much darker thorax, nearly black. Can't be a trico, not fat enough. Net some more naturals. Ha, a spinner now, with a tiny black segment at the very tip of the abdomen, and a black thorax. Better change flies." The trouble was, I didn't have any flies that looked like the naturals. I did have a Pale Olive Spinner, but it didn't work.

I looked this one up in my fly books. As near as I could tell it was a *Paraleptophlebia mollis*. The trouble is, I couldn't find the mollis listed in any of my books as a western hatch. I asked Ed Engle, who has spent more time on the South Platte than anyone I know, and he said, "Yeah, I know, I've seen them too. They used to be found miles downstream. They must be migrating upstream." Months later, I spoke about mayfly migration with a stream entomologist who agreed with Ed and me that, based on our description, the natural probably was the mollis. He also confirmed a suspicion I've held for a long time, that once a stream gets dammed (that is to say a dam is built on it), the stretch below the dam becomes a new stream in geologic terms, with rapid changes in aquatic life that continue for many years. This could be as little as five or as many as a hundred years. A hundred years in the life of a stream is hardly a blink in geologic time.

This could explain the sudden appearance of the phlebs miles upstream from where they used to occur, but it didn't answer the nagging questions, "How did the *P. mollis* get there in the first place if it's an eastern hatch?" and "If it isn't the mollis, what is it?" Perhaps it's questions like these that drive folks to become entomologists.

At any rate, the important things we need to know about this particular mayfly are that both duns and spinners have very pale olive bodies and dark thoraxes; the dun has pale gray wings, while the spinner has a tiny charcoal-colored segment near its tails; and they both come in sizes 18 and 20.

I tied some Paraleptophlebia Duns and Spinners before the season was over, and I am happy to report that both patterns worked wonderfully. My humiliation lasted only a few days, until I was armed with the correct pattern. But I relearned an important lesson about taking nature for granted, and thinking I knew which mayflies were hatching without bothering to check.

Paraleptophlebia dun (photo by Ted Fauceglia)

Paraleptophlebia spinner

Paraleptophlebia Quill Dun

Paraleptophlebia Quill Parachute

Paraleptophlebia Quill Spinner

NOTE: See chapter 18 for detailed tying instructions for quill-bodied flies.

PARALEPTOPHLEBIA QUILL DUN

Hook: Mustad 94840 or Tiemco 100, #20 and #18.

Thread: Danville's 6/0 #61 light olive.

Tail: Smoky dun spade hackle fibers, length to equal entire hook.

Body: One stripped and very light olive dyed rooster hackle quill. Use weak Rit kelly green.

Thorax: Fine charcoal gray dubbing. Use only two very fine turns.

Wings: Light medium dun hen hackle tips.

Hackle: Light dun hackle

PARALEPTOPHLEBIA QUILL PARACHUTE

Use the same pattern as for the Dun, except use a white turkey T-base feather segment for the wing post.

PARALEPTOPHLEBIA QUILL SPINNER

Hook: Same as Dun.

Thread: Danville's 6/0 #1 white.

Tail: White spade hackle fibers, length to equal entire hook plus one hook-eye distance.

Body: For tip of abdomen, three or four turns of black 6/0 tying thread. Immediately in front of the black tip, tie in one very pale green rooster neck hackle quill. The color should be nearly white, with hints of pale green. *Do not* tie in the tailing fibers with black tying thread; it will show through the light-colored quill and change the color of the body. Use the black thread only as a tag to the rear of the abdomen.

Wings: Pair of white hen hackle tips.

Thorax: Fine charcoal or black dubbing figure-eight wrapped around and between wings.

ELEVEN

Pale Morning Duns

If the blue-winged olive is my favorite hatch, I'd have to say the pale morning dun is my second favorite hatch. It's usually a daylight hatch; also, the flies we use to imitate the insects lumped into the PMD category are relatively easy to tie, and their light color makes them easy to see on the water. I love to fish a PMD along a shady bank, where it would be almost impossible to see a dull-colored blue-winged olive. On certain stretches of many streams, pale morning duns are on the water for several weeks. In the West, where streams begin at 12,000 or 13,000 feet and begin to flatten at around five thousand feet, a fly fisher can fish the same hatch for several more weeks simply by following it upstream. "Upstream" takes on a whole new connotation in this case. It doesn't mean just a 20-mile stretch of stream; we're dealing with a vertical drop of 8,000 feet—a mile and half straight down! It's white water you can't stand up in; it's riffles, bends, pools, glides, and meadows. Some of it might be between two canyon walls so steep you need to hike a mile or more to get back to a spot where you can actually stand in the water again. Some of it flows through boggy meadows and spreads into a half-dozen tiny rivulets. No matter the type of water you'll find trout, and they're usually eager to eat a dry fly.

You'll certainly find blue-winged olives through the entire course of the stream. You'll also find pale morning duns, which often hatch with the blue-winged olives in alternating waves. The trout will switch from one to the other without hesitation, but if you don't change flies with the hatch, you'll go fishless. A situation like this makes for some wonderful fly fishing, but you'd better not carry just one PMD pattern. Of all the mayflies, PMDs seem to be the most variable in coloration. On the Frying Pan, for instance, the PMDs near Ruedi Dam have very green, prominently segmented bodies with tinges of gray and bronze, and hints of yellow in the wings. They are an easy-to-see sizes 14 or 16. Just four miles downstream, the PMDs are still sizes 14 and 16, but they have cream bodies ribbed with what I call "old rose pink" (a mix of tan and pink); the legs and tails have changed from medium dun/bronze to golden ginger; and the wings have become pale creamy yellow. I don't know anyone who has seen this PMD anywhere but the Pan, yet the pattern catches fish on many streams with PMD hatches. You can catch some trout with either fly in both stretches of the Pan, but you'll catch a lot more if the color of your fly matches the natural. The Frying Pan below Ruedi is a tailwater stream, which means it is usually very clear. It also gets fished very hard, and all the trout have been caught at least once. Trout seem to get quite finicky in such situations, and you'd be wise to be just as finicky about your fly tying and purchasing.

The two PMD color phases may be two different species of mayflies that happen to hatch at the same time; or they could be due to the Pan's trip through a red rock canyon changing the stream chemistry and altering the insects' colors so dramatically as to make them appear to be different species. Most of the downstream aquatic insects on the Pan (caddis especially) have a touch of orange in their bodies and wings. Incorporating some of these subtle color variations in a fly can often mean the difference between a good day's catch or a frustrating day of refusal rises and a few small fish. This is particularly true with a mid-summer daytime hatch. We like to fish then because it's easier to see the fly, but the trout can see our fly much better as well, and will refuse anything less than a near perfect match.

The common PMD, so plentiful on many streams from west to east, has a light ginger tail and legs, as well as a body that is basically ginger but with tinges of tan and/or light olive, and/or light gray, and/or light pink. Occasionally you'll find PMDs with bodies containing tinges of all those colors. The wings are usually creamy yellow with a tinge of light bronze or light gray. Anywhere you find them, PMDs are beautiful insects, somehow seeming more delicate than other mayflies of the same size.

Frying Pan PMD, light olive

Frying Pan PMD Quill Dun, light olive

Frying Pan PMD Quill Parachute, light olive

Frying Pan PMD dun, pink

Frying Pan PMD Quill Dun, pink

Frying Pan PMD Quill Parachute, pink

Standard PMD dun, ginger

Standard PMD Quill Dun

Standard PMD Quill Parachute

NOTE: See chapter 18 for detailed tying instructions for quill-bodied flies.

FRYING PAN PMD QUILL DUN, LIGHT OLIVE

   Hook: Mustad 94840 or Tiemco 100, #18, #16, #14.

Thread: Danville's 6/0 #61 light olive.

   Tail: Light medium dun spade hackle fibers, length to equal entire hook.

  Body: Stripped and light olive dyed rooster hackle quill.

 Wings: Yellow and dun hen hackle tips. Dye first to pale yellow, then overdye with weak gray; this allows the yellow to show through at the base of each hackle feather.

Hackle: Medium dun hackle.

FRYING PAN PMD QUILL DUN, PINK

Hook: Mustad 94840 or Tiemco 100, #18, #16, #14.

Thread: Danville's 6/0 #41 beige.

Tail: Golden ginger spade hackle fibers, length to equal entire hook.

Body: Pink-and-tan-dyed stripped rooster hackle quills. Dye first with Rit pink, then overdye with Rit tan. You should have a tan quill with pink showing through.

Wings: Creamy dun hen hackle tips. Dye first to dark cream with weak Rit tan, then overdye with weak Rit gray. Pull the neck from the dye the moment you see the gray begin to penetrate the feathers.

Hackle: Golden ginger hackle.

STANDARD PMD QUILL DUN

Hook: Mustad 94840 or Tiemco 100, #18, #16, #14.

Thread: Danville's 6/0 #41 beige.

Tail: Medium ginger spade hackle fibers, length to equal entire hook.

Body: Stripped and dyed rooster neck hackle quills. Dye first with light Rit tan then overdye with light Rit kelly green or pink.

Wings: Dyed hen hackle tips. Dye first to a dark cream with light Rit tan, then overdye with weak Rit gray. Pull the neck from the dye the moment you see the gray begin to penetrate the edges of each feather.

Hackle: Medium ginger hackle.

PARACHUTES FOR ABOVE PATTERNS

Use a white turkey T-base feather segment as a wing post, in place of the dun patterns' hen hackle wings. See chapter 18 for tying instructions for parachutes.

QUILL-BODIED SPINNERS

Tie the same pattern listed for the Blue-winged Olive.

TWELVE

Red Quills

Three patterns will pretty much cover the red quill hatches no matter whether you're fishing eastern or western waters. Actually, there's only one pattern, but its tail and hackle come in three different color variations. Hook sizes range from as large as 12 to as small as 20. The Red Quill pattern covers a wide variety of mayflies—some are imitations of male duns, while others are imitations of female duns of another species. Throw in the confusion of the upright-winged spinner and you have at least a dozen or more of some quite important hatches pretty well covered. The Red Quill is a fly you should have in your fly box at all times and in a wide range of sizes. I often use it when I run out of the right size of Blue-winged Olive, Blue Dun, Ginger Quill, or Pale Morning Dun. It doesn't work quite as well as a more specific imitation, but it is better than not fishing, and the trout will eat it when they're feeding heavily. This is especially true on cloudy or overcast days, when the trout seem to lose a little of their caution. A Red Quill Parachute is an excellent search pattern when there is no hatch but you don't feel like sitting on the bank for an hour or two waiting for one to begin. I have caught a lot of nice trout at times like that. Evidently, they didn't want to wait an hour or two either.

I have found the Red Quill pattern very effective from as early as late May to as late as early October. If you were to limit your fly selection to only a few patterns, you would be wise to include the Red Quill.

Note: See chapter 18 for detailed tying instructions for quill-bodied flies.

RED QUILL, DUN HACKLE

Hook: Mustad 94840 or Tiemco 100, #20-#12.

Thread: Danville's 6/0 #60 olive, or #100 black (I prefer the olive).

Tail: Medium dun spade hackle fibers, length to equal entire hook.

Body: Stripped and light brown dyed rooster neck hackles, 7"-8" in length: two for size 16 and larger; one for size 18 and smaller.

Wings: Pair of medium dun hen hackle tips.

Hackle: Medium dun hackle: two for size 14 and larger; one for size 16 and smaller.

RED QUILL, BROWN HACKLE

Use the same recipe as above, except substitute brown spade hackle for the tailing, and brown hackle for the hackle collar.

RED QUILL, GINGER HACKLE

Hook: Same as Dun.

Thread: Danville's 6/0 #41 beige.

Tail: Ginger spade hackle fibers, length to equal entire hook.

Body: Stripped and light brown dyed rooster neck hackle quills, 7"-8" in length: two for size 16 and larger; one for size 18 and smaller.

Wings: Pair of light dun hen hackle tips.

Hackle: Ginger hackle: two for size 14 and larger; one for size 16 and smaller.

Red quill dun

Red quill spinner (photo by John Gierach)

Red Quill, Dun Hackle

Red Quill, Brown Hackle

Red Quill, Ginger Hackle

Red Quill Parachute

Parachute patterns are tied exactly the same; use a segment of white turkey T-base feather for the wing post.

The spinner pattern for the Red Quill is the same as the Red Quill Spinner pattern listed for Blue-winged Olives.

THIRTEEN

Tricos

It used to be called the "white-winged black." Many of us know it today as the "trik" or "trico." To the entomologists it's the *Tricorythodes*. Whatever you call it, this tiny mayfly can provide either fantastic fishing or utter frustration. Tricos exist in profuse numbers on nearly all trout streams from coast to coast. The researchers tell us that the males begin hatching at night, the females in the early morning. They rarely live more than 24 hours as winged adults. The hatch can last for weeks, even months, with thousands of tricos hatching at a time. The heavy spinner fall can literally blanket the water, with the spinners coming downstream in clumps of a dozen or more. A few fly tyers have developed patterns to imitate clumps of tricos. I've managed to avoid that so far by catching the hatch early and late in the season, when there are fewer naturals to contend with. It may sound a little ultrapurist, but I prefer fishing a fly imitating one insect at time.

Another way to avoid the heavy spinner fall is to begin fishing very early in the morning, at first gray light. There will be some duns on the water then, and the fish are already looking up and eating them. There are far fewer fishermen around as well, and you will probably enjoy an hour or two of solitude before the gang shows up for the spinner fall. If you fish the duns early you'll probably catch as many fish during the hatch as you would during the spinner fall. You'll also be able to see your upright-winged fly a lot easier than you could a flat-winged spinner among hundreds of naturals. The trout will find it easier to see as well. When the spinner fall is about over and the gang begins to leave, start looking for what I call a "spooky riser"—a trout holding and feeding in a place that everyone has overlooked. It may well be the biggest trout you've seen all summer. Look for an undercut bank with or without grass hanging over the stream, or for a small triangle of shadow on the water caused by a small stone or stump. There will be a trout there, holding in about four inches of water not more than six or eight inches from the bank. Watch the water, scanning back and forth continuously. These trout have learned that it's safe to hang out in such places because they don't get bothered much. If they see some two-legged monster sloshing through the stream too close to them, they merely slide into deeper water until the coast is clear. These fish have been feeding throughout the spinner fall, and will continue to feed on spinners until long after the last natural has disappeared, because their feeding station is such that they hardly have to move in order to ingest another trico.

Prospecting for spooky risers is a good technique to use during other hatches as well, but I find it most effective during the trico spinner fall. The smaller trout that have been so obvious throughout the heavier part of the spinner fall are holding in heavier current, coming to the surface only when it's worthwhile—to eat four or five spinners at a time—then returning to their lies behind rocks. When the spinner fall begins to taper off, many of these fish simply stop feeding because it isn't worth spending energy to rise all the way to the surface for only one tiny insect.

The trico ranges in size from 18 to as small as 24. You should carry duns, parachutes, and spinner patterns in all those sizes. But just having the correct size doesn't mean you'll catch many fish. You must be able to present the fly so that it floats down to a rising trout exactly over the center of his nose! Remember, tricos are very small, and there are thousands of them on the water at any given time during the spinner fall. The trout seem to know they don't have to move far to get a meal.

If you have the right-sized fly, you'll catch the fish. If you're not getting any rises, either your tippet is too heavy and won't allow the fly to

Trico dun

Trico dun

Trico spinner (photo by Dave Hughes)

Trico Quill Dun

Trico Quill Parachute

Trico Quill Spinner

float freely, or you're simply not presenting the fly over the fish's nose. This is often the case in any hatch, and the first two questions you should ask yourself after you are satisfied that you have the correct pattern are: "Is the tippet fine and limp enough?" and "Is the fly directly over the fish?"

NOTE: See chapter 18 for detailed tying instructions for the following patterns.

TRICO QUILL DUN

   Hook: Mustad 94840 or 94842 (turned-up eye), or Tiemco 100 or 101 (ringed eye).

Thread: Danville's #1 white for tailing and quill body, and Danville's #100 black for thorax, wing, and hackle; or Uni-Thread 8/0 white and black.

   Tail: Small clump (four or five) white spade hackle fibers, length to equal 1½ times entire hook.

  Body: One stripped and pale green dyed rooster hackle quill. Be careful to save room for one or two turns of thorax dubbing, wings, and hackle.

Thorax: Tie in black thread; clip off white thread and black tag. On size 18 and 20 flies, dub a very small amount of very fine black dubbing over the tie-down area of the quill body. On size 20 and smaller, use the black thread to create the black thorax of the natural.

 Wings: Pair of pure white hen hackle tips, one size larger than hook (size 18 wings on a size 20 hook).

Hackle: One black rooster hackle.

TRICO QUILL PARACHUTE

Same as above, except use a segment of white turkey T-base feather for a wing post.

TRICO QUILL SPINNER

   Hook: Same as Dun.

Thread: Danville's 6/0 #100 black, or Uni-Thread 8/0 black.

NOTE: Since the spinner's body is black, there's no need for white thread on the spinner pattern.

Tail: Small clump (four or five) white spade hackle fibers, length to equal twice the entire hook. I tie some even longer.

Body: One stripped and black-dyed rooster neck hackle quill, or two black moose mane hairs for size 18, one for size 20. For size 22 and smaller, I use black tying thread for the body.

Wings: Pair of pure white hen hackle tips one size larger than hook (as noted in Dun pattern).

Thorax: Fine black dubbing. Create a thorax at least two or three times the diameter of the abdomen.

FOURTEEN

Caddis Flies

If we could conduct a nationwide survey of fly fishers to determine the most important fly type for the entire year, I'd be willing to bet money the answer would be "mayfly." If we were to ask "What pattern is the most fun to fish?" I suspect the answer would be "caddis fly." Caddis patterns float like tiny corks; they're extremely durable, highly visible, and easy to tie; their materials are readily available; and trout often take them with rises best described as vicious. Caddis fly hatches seem to occur throughout the summer, which can include late spring and early fall, and nearly every trout stream from coast to coast has a caddis population.

I've seen caddis hatches that were so sparse no trout would look at one. I've also seen a caddis hatch so heavy that, when I opened my mouth to tell my friend John Gierach I was going to quit fishing for awhile because I couldn't see my fly on the water, caddis flies flew into my mouth. This was on the Henry's Fork in Idaho, directly across the highway from Mike Lawson's Fly Shop. The stream was covered with caddis flies to a density of about thirty flies per square foot of surface, and the water was literally boiling with rising trout. Some die-hard fishermen covered their noses and mouths with bandanas to keep the little caddis out. At times like this, fishing is simply a useless effort. Even if you have a perfect match for the natural, you can't see your artificial on the water, and what chance do you have of a trout eating your artificial with thirty or more naturals per square foot? It means I'm going to have to make at least thirty casts before I might get a strike. When the trout are boiling the surface I can't make thirty casts without getting a strike. My frustration factor skyrockets off the chart, and the best thing I can do is go sit on the bank and watch the show.

Fortunately, we only need to know how to tie a few basic patterns to imitate most caddis flies. If you can tie a dubbed body, a down-hair wing, and a hackle collar, you can tie any adult caddis; it's only a matter of color and size variations.

My favorite pattern is one I call the St. Vrain Caddis, because I developed this pale-yellow-and-cream fly to imitate what used to be a consistently heavy hatch on the stream across the road from John Gierach's house. There aren't nearly as many caddis now as there were ten years ago, but some bugs are still there; more importantly, I have caught trout on this pattern from Colorado to Montana to Vermont to Labrador. It's a hot fly and I wouldn't be without some. The St. Vrain Caddis contains some very specific colors, but the pattern can be easily altered to whatever colors imitate the caddis in your favorite stream. I prefer the hackle-collared pattern to the palmer-hackled, because I think it's a little easier to twitch a hackle-collared fly without drowning it.

Yellow caddis adult

Olive caddis adult (photo by John Gierach)

St.Vrain Caddis,Yellow   *St.Vrain Caddis, Olive*

NOTE: See chapter 18 for detailed tying instructions for the following patterns.

ST. VRAIN CADDIS, YELLOW

Hook: Mustad 94840 or Tiemco 100, #16-#12. Use loop eye or turned-up eye hooks for size 18 and smaller.

Thread: Danville's 6/0 #8, yellow, or Uni-Thread 8/0 light cahill.

Body: *Very fine* dry-fly dubbing (beaver or rabbit), dyed or blended to *pale* yellow. Create a reverse-tapered body so that the hair wing isn't forced up by a dramatic shoulder, as in mayfly patterns.

Hair Wing: Small clump of blond elk or bleached deer body hair (*no* tip markings), length to extend past hook bend by half hook-gap distance. Make the wing rather sparse. You should easily see the body of the fly through the hair wing.

Hackle Collar: Your stiffest light ginger, tied a little on the dense side.

This is excellent during the little yellow stonefly hatch, provided the wing isn't too bushy. Tie this same pattern with light tan dubbing for other light-colored caddis hatches.

ST. VRAIN CADDIS, OLIVE

Hook: As above.

Thread: Danville's 6/0 olive, or Uni-Thread 8/0 olive.

Body: *Very fine* dry-fly dubbing (beaver or rabbit), dyed or blended to golden olive. Create a reverse-tapered body to prevent the hair wing from being forced up.

Wing: Small clump of natural dark brown elk body hair, length to
extend past hook bend by half hook-gap distance.

Hackle Collar: Your stiffest brown dry-fly hackle.

NOTE: Substitute medium brown dubbing for the golden olive for another
very effective caddis pattern.

By now I'm sure you have thought of some color variations of your
own. Be careful to observe the body-to-wing length ratios of the naturals, however. The hair wing lengths above are approximate for most
caddis flies, but there are a few whose wings are fully three times their
body length. An artificial's silhouette is important to the success of any
fly, and is too often ignored with caddis patterns. Don't extend the wing
too far beyond the bend of the hook, however; a rising trout's nose could
push your fly away! A good rule of thumb is that no part of a caddis
should extend beyond the bend of the hook more than twice the hook-
gap distance.

SPENT CADDIS

I carry only two patterns for the spent caddis—a Spent Cream Caddis,
and a Spent Olive Caddis. Both are tied from size 18 through 22, and
are simplified versions of the Spent Microcaddis that Mike and Sheralee
Lawson developed in the late 1970s. This little fly has become an indis-
pensable member of my caddis fly box. Not only is it a good imitation
of tiny caddis hatches, but it also doubles as a small beetle.

Spent Cream Caddis

NOTE: See chapter 18 for detailed tying instructions for the following patterns.

SPENT CREAM CADDIS

   Hook: Mustad 94842 or Tiemco 101, #22, #20, #18.

  Thread: Danville's 6/0 #8 yellow, or Uni-Thread 8/0 light cahill.

   Body: *Very fine* dry-fly dubbing (beaver or rabbit), natural or dyed and blended to pale cream. The body has a very thin profile with a reversed taper.

  Wings: One hen pheasant clear blond breast feather tip, tied flat as described for the Little Yellow Stone fly wing, in chapter 18.

 Hackle: One light ginger dry-fly hackle, collar style.

NOTE 1: The Lawson pattern calls for two feather tips for the wing, and a peacock thorax.

NOTE 2: This fly sometimes fishes better with all the hackle on the bottom of the fly clipped off even with the thorax. Leave the top for visibility.

Spent Olive Caddis

SPENT OLIVE CADDIS

   Hook: Mustad 94842 or Tiemco 101, #22, #20, #18.

  Thread: Danville's 6/0 #60 olive, or #100 black; or Uni-Thread 8/0 black, camel, or olive.

Body: *Very fine* dry-fly dubbing (beaver or rabbit), dyed or blended to golden olive. The body has a very thin profile with a reversed taper.

Wings: One mottled brown hen neck hackle feather tip, or ruffed grouse body feather tip, tied flat, as for the Little Yellow Stonefly (see chapter 18).

Hackle: One medium brown hackle, collar style.

NOTE: This fly is sometimes more effective if all the hackle is clipped from the bottom.

CADDIS LARVAE

Have you ever seen a caddis larva with a fuzzy body? I mean the live, natural bug? Neither have I. Yet every caddis larva imitation in every fly shop in the country has a dubbed body. There have been a few attempts to use latex strips for caddis larva bodies, but latex seems to self-destruct in the fly box. A dozen or more dubbing blends have come on the market in as many years that claim to be the ultimate answer for all our dubbing needs. If anyone tries to convince you of this, turn around and walk away. Nothing could be farther from the truth. A "market the sparkle" philosophy seems to run rampant through the fly-fishing industry these days. The newer man-made dubbing materials are marketed as having "Improved Translucence," "Ultra Translucence;" or as "Ultra-fine," "Super Fine," and on and on. Pick up any package of dubbing at your favorite fly shop and you'll see what I mean. Ask yourself, "Ultra from what?" "Improved from what?" "Super over what?" I can understand "Improved," because according to Webster, all that means is "to enhance in value or quality." Simply raising the price could be interpreted as enhancing the value. Super? Webster says *super* means "over and above" or "higher in quantity, quality, or degree than." Putting a pinch more dubbing in a bag makes it super. Webster defines *ultra* as "going beyond others or beyond due limit." Everyone can't be going beyond others, though, and just what exactly is the due limit? But here's the kicker. *Translucent* means "permitting the passage of light." Translucency is "something that is transparent!" It sounds like we're being encouraged to use materials that will not only make a fly fuzzier, but allow the trout to see the hook as well!

So what's the point? Simply this: Caddis fly larvae are not fuzzy. Their prominently segmented bodies reflect a lot of light, but they are not transparent. I understand that the idea of adding sparkle fibers to a dubbing mix is to give the appearance of translucence, but when we win the translucence battle, we lose the war of creating a realistic silhouette. Dubbed bodies are invariably too fat and fuzzy. Nymph, larva, and pupa imitations are presented to the trout at their eye level. Why not use a material that more accurately simulates the natural? Why not use a material that is easier and faster to tie? A material that you can dye to any color imaginable. Why not use stripped and dyed rooster hackle quills or dyed wild turkey biots?

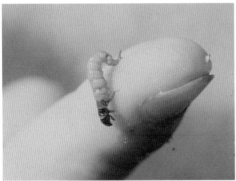

Caddis larva

Caddis Quill Larva

NOTE: See chapter 18 for detailed tying instructions for this pattern.

CADDIS QUILL LARVA

Hook: Mustad 3906 or 3906B or Tiemco 200R, #18-#12.

Thread: Danville's 6/0, or Uni-Thread; color to match body.

Body: Stripped and dyed 7"-8" rooster butt hackle quill.

Hackle: Ostrich, dyed appropriate color (black or brown). Clip off the top fibers.

Head: Brown or black.

CADDIS PUPAE

I've tried to improve Gary LaFontaine's Caddis Pupa patterns dozens of times, and I cannot. They are as near perfect as artificials can be without impaling naturals on bare hooks. Follow his tying instructions and material requirements very carefully and you'll have Caddis Pupae for all your needs. Be very careful to tie them a little on the sparse side. They're moving, subsurface flies, and will not behave like naturals if they're dressed heavily.

FIFTEEN

Midges

In states with no closed season on trout fishing, midges offer the fly fisher at least *something* to do during the winter, when the mayflies, caddis, and stoneflies seem to be hibernating. At least that's how many people look at midge fishing. I view it a little differently. Many western streams have midge hatches almost daily throughout the winter. In fact, if you watch the air and water very carefully, you'll soon discover there are midge hatches nearly every month of the year, especially on natural spring creeks and cold tailwaters. Many fly fishers overlook this and continue to fish a mayfly emerger or spinner when the trout are actually feeding on a more plentiful midge hatch. This doesn't happen very often because the trout are more apt to feed on (usually) much-larger mayflies. I know some folks leave their midge boxes at home during the summer, when the mayfly royalty begins to appear, but I always carry mine; it has saved me from humiliation more than once.

Most folks hear the word "midge" and immediately think of tiny, 20- to 26-size flies that spend most of their time in your ears and behind your glasses. To many, a midge is any aquatic insect that is tiny, or tiny and black. For the past twenty years, however, articles and books on the subject have told us midges belong to the order *Diptera*, genus *Chironomus* (I looked this up). Despite all this published information, there still seems to be some confusion, because there are fly shop catalogues that list a size-20 Adams—complete with upright, divided wings—as a midge. Some catalogues list a midge as a small fly with tails(!), a body, and hackle, but no wing. Yet a true midge has no tail. Its wings are generally straight back and flat, not upright and divided like a mayfly's, and its legs are longer and thinner than a mayfly's.

I suspect the term "midge" was originally an abbreviation form of "midget" and applied to any aquatic insect smaller than size 16. Some literature pictures midges as dry flies size 18 and smaller. We now know some of these to be blue-winged olives and microcaddis, for example. I have seen a large (size 16), gray midge in flight that looked exactly like a size-16 BWO. Its legs were so long that, when folded back for flight, they looked like the tail fibers of a mayfly dun. The first time I encountered this hatch, I fished Olive Quill Duns and Blue Quill Duns to no avail. It was only after netting the insect that I noticed it wasn't a mayfly but a very large gray midge. Which brings up a point: You're imitating how an insect appears on the *water*, not in the air or on a rock or tree branch. For example, some midges run about the surface in short three- to four-inch bursts of energy, their legs and wings a blur. The trout often will feed only on the moving midges, not on the dead drifts. A suitable pattern for such midges should probably incorporate grizzly hackle and a hackle fiber wing, both of which give the illusion of movement. We should never assume that an insect we view in flight will appear the same to the trout when the insect is on the stream's surface.

In his ground-breaking book, *Matching the Hatch* (Macmillan, 1955), Ernie Schwiebert states that there are more than 16,000 species of *Diptera* in North America, about a fifth of which are aquatic. A stream entomologist I know said that "there are over 3,000 species of aquatic midges in North America—that we know of." That's a lot of insects to try to imitate. I've narrowed this number down considerably to four color patterns that I tie in about four sizes, from size 18 down to 24, and occasionally a size 26. This works for the midges on the waters I fish most. You may discover some minor color variations on your home waters, but I think the patterns listed below will give most of you a head start on getting a little closer to the natural's appearance.

ADULTS

Black midge adult (photo by Ted Fauceglia)

Dun midge adult (photo by Ted Fauceglia)

Olive midge adult (photo by Ted Fauceglia)

Cream midge adult (photo by Ted Fauceglia)

Black Quill Midge Adult

Dun Quill Midge Adult

Olive Quill Midge Adult   *Cream Quill Midge Adult*

NOTE: See chapter 18 for detailed tying instructions for the following patterns.

BLACK QUILL MIDGE ADULT

Hook: Mustad 94842 (turned-up eye) or Tiemco 100 or 101 (ringed eye), #26-#18.

Thread: Danville's 6/0 #100 black, or Uni-Thread 8/0 black.

Tail: None.

Body: One stripped and black-dyed rooster hackle quill.

Wings: Plastic strip, length to extend one hook-gap distance beyond the end of the hook bend. See chapter 18 for tying instructions for this material.

Hackle: One black hackle feather.

DUN QUILL MIDGE ADULT

Hook: Mustad 94842 (turned-up eye) or Tiemco 100 or 101 (ringed eye), #26-#18.

Thread: Danville's 6/0 #31 gray, or Uni-Thread 8/0 gray.

Tail: None.

Body: One stripped and medium dun-dyed rooster neck hackle quill.

Wings: Same as Black Midge Quill.

Hackle: One medium dun hackle.

OLIVE QUILL MIDGE ADULT

Hook: Mustad 94842 (turned-up eye) or Tiemco 100 or 101 (ringed eye), #26-#18.

Thread: Danville's 6/0 #61 bright green, or Uni-Thread 8/0 light cahill.

Tail: None.

Body: One stripped and light green dyed rooster neck hackle quill.

Wings: Same as Black Midge Quill.

Hackle: One medium dun hackle.

CREAM QUILL MIDGE ADULT

Hook: Mustad 94842 (turned-up eye) or Tiemco 100 or 101 (ringed eye), #26-#18.

Thread: Danville's 6/0 #41 beige, or Uni-Thread 8/0 light cahill.

Tail: None.

Body: One stripped and cream-dyed light ginger rooster neck hackle quill.

Wings: Same as Black Midge Quill.

Hackle: One light ginger hackle.

LARVAE

I'm breaking with tradition and presenting my midge patterns beginning with the adult instead of the larva. I don't like fishing the tiny larva patterns all that much, and I don't much enjoy nymph fishing either, although I'll do both if I have to. "Have to" means that no trout are rising for miles, and they haven't done so for days. I have some midge larva patterns, but I'm not sure I can call them "mine." They are so simple, I figure someone else must have thought of them long ago.

Note that, although the following midge larva patterns are identified by color, you shouldn't associate them with the colors of the adults, since there are occasions when adult colors are dramatically different from those of the larvae. Net the water to discover the color of the natural larvae.

Midge larva

Black Quill Midge Larva

Dun Quill Midge Larva

Brown Quill Midge Larva

Cream Quill Midge Larva

NOTE: See chapter 18 for detailed tying instructions for the following patterns.

BLACK QUILL MIDGE LARVA

Hook: Mustad 94842 (turned-up eye) or Tiemco 100 or 101 (ringed eye), #26–#18.

Thread: Danville's 6/0 #100 black, or Uni-Thread 8/0 black.

Tail: None.

Body: One stripped and black-dyed rooster neck hackle quill, or two black moose mane hairs for size 18 and 20, one for size 22 and smaller.

Thorax: One or two turns of loosely dubbed black-dyed Australian 'possum.

DUN QUILL MIDGE LARVA

Hook: Same as Black Quill Larva.

Thread: Danville's #100 black, Uni-Thread 8/0 black.

Tail: None.

Body: One stripped and dark dun-dyed rooster hackle quill, or two dark dun moose mane hairs for size 18 and 20, one for size 22 and smaller.

Thorax: One or two turns of loosely dubbed dark dun-dyed Australian 'possum.

BROWN QUILL MIDGE LARVA

Hook: Same as Black Quill Larva.

Thread: Danville's #100 black, or Uni-Thread 8/0 black.

Tail: None.

Body: One stripped and dark brown (coachman brown) dyed rooster neck hackle quill.

Thorax: One or two turns of loosely dubbed dark brown dyed Australian 'possum.

CREAM QUILL MIDGE LARVA

Hook: Same as Black Quill Larva.

Thread: Danville's 6/0 #41 beige, or Uni-Thread 8/0 light cahill.

Tail: None.

Body: One stripped and light ginger dyed rooster neck hackle quill, or two ginger-colored moose mane hairs for size 18 and 20, one for size 22 and smaller.

Thorax: One or two turns of loosely dubbed dark amber dyed Australian 'possum.

EMERGERS

The emerger stage of any aquatic insect is that time when the adult is in the process of leaving the nymph case. This event usually occurs at the surface of the stream, but can occur at the stream bottom (some mayflies), or on the stream bank (some stoneflies). Many have written that midge pupae hang vertically in the surface film during emergence, but I haven't seen this—perhaps because the streams I fish regularly have few vertical-hanging midges. All the common midge emergers on those streams lie horizontally in the surface film while the adult crawls straight forward out of the pupal husk. This produces a silhouette that is considerably longer than either the nymph or the adult—something to keep in mind when you're tying the emerging midge. The one exception I've found is a size 18 to 20 dun midge on the Frying Pan River that emerges straight up! The wings and legs are held tightly to the body as it rapidly emerges from the nymph case, which is horizontal at the surface. The trout key in on this activity and make rather splashy rises in their attempts to eat the bugs before they get away.

My favorite material for the trailing shuck of a midge emerger (and many mayfly emergers) is mallard flank, either natural gray or tan-dyed. The prominent natural barring of the fibers nicely simulates the segmentation of the natural's body, and it has just the right amount of light-reflecting qualities and a certain amount of translucence. It takes only four or five fibers to create the illusion of a trailing empty nymph case. Select a large mallard flank with an off-center quill. The feather fibers on one side of the quill will be quite thin and wispy; the fibers on the other side will be noticeably thicker and quite straight. Use the thicker fibers, but not too many. You're imitating a trailing *empty* nymph case. Antron yarn fibers are a popular material for trailing nymph shucks on emerger patterns, but I don't like it. It has too much sparkle, and the fibers don't stay together in the water. An empty nymph case is very thin and sparkles only when you hold it up in the air to look at it. Trout don't feed at chest-high altitudes.

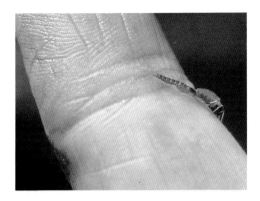

Midge emerger

Black Quill Midge Emerger

Dun Quill Midge Emerger

Olive Quill Midge Emerger

Cream Quill Midge Emerger

NOTE: See chapter 18 for detailed tying instructions for the following patterns.

BLACK QUILL MIDGE EMERGER

Hook: Mustad 94842 (turned-up eye) or Tiemco 100 or 101 (ringed eye), #26-#18.

Thread: Danville's 6/0 #100 black, or Uni-Thread 8/0 black.

Shuck: Four or five tan-dyed mallard flank feather fibers, length to equal entire hook. Dye to the color of wood duck flank with Rit tan.

Body: One stripped and black-dyed rooster hackle quill.

Wings: Plastic strip (see chapter 18). Trim the wing on the emerger at a point even with the end of the hook bend. Trim the corners of the clipped wing.

Hackle: One black rooster hackle.

DUN QUILL MIDGE EMERGER

Hook: As above.

Thread: Danville's 6/0 #31 gray, or Uni-Thread 8/0 gray.

Shuck: Four or five fibers of natural gray mallard flank feather, length to equal entire hook.

Body: One stripped and medium dun-dyed rooster hackle quill.

Wings: Plastic strip (see chapter 18). Trim the wing on the emerger at a point even with the end of the hook bend. Trim the corners of the clipped wing.

Hackle: One medium dun rooster hackle.

OLIVE QUILL MIDGE EMERGER

Hook: As above.

Thread: Danville's 6/0 #61 bright green, or Uni-Thread 8/0 light cahill.

Shuck: Four or five fibers of natural gray mallard flank length to equal entire hook.

Body: One stripped and light green dyed rooster hackle quill.

Wings: Plastic strip (see chapter 18). Trim the wing on the emerger at a point even with the end of the hook bend. Trim the corners of the clipped wing.

Hackles: One medium dun rooster hackle.

CREAM QUILL MIDGE EMERGER

Hook: As above.

Thread: Danville's 6/0 #41 beige, or Uni-Thread 8/0 light cahill.

Shuck: Four or five fibers of mallard flank feather, length to equal entire hook. Dye to the color of the wood duck flank with Rit tan.

Body: One stripped and light cream (or light ginger) dyed rooster neck hackle quill.

Wings: Plastic strip (see chapter 18). Trim the wing at a point even with the end of the bend of the hook. Trim the corners of the clipped wing.

Hackle: One light ginger rooster hackle.

Sometimes it's a good idea to trim all the hackle flush with the thorax area on the bottom of the emerger pattern to let it rest a little more heavily on the surface. I normally don't do this until I'm on the stream and find it's something I can do to make the fly a little more effective. Grease the trailing shuck and the forward portion of the fly with a good silicone paste flotant. This will cause the pattern to float horizontally in the surface film. On those days when your fingers are too cold to tie good knots and you want to change from emerger to adult, simply clip off the trailing shuck and you have an instant adult midge pattern.

SIXTEEN

Stoneflies

The giant western salmon fly, or willow fly, is the stonefly that seems to get most of the attention of a lot of writers, fly tyers, and fly fishers. I think this is partly because its hatch comes early in the spring, after a long cold winter of waiting for something to begin happening on our favorite streams. In many respects, the salmon fly hatch signifies the start of what we all hope and dream will be a glorious year of dry-fly fishing. The huge adults bring ravenous rises from trout of all sizes; the artificials are easy to see on the water, and we can fish heavier tippets, make longer (often sloppier) casts, and in general work out the kinks in our wading and casting skills. It's a time when we find that there are new leaks in our waders, that we really should have bought a new fly line, and that a small bank fire can produce more heat than our home furnaces.

STONEFLY NYMPHS

Not many fly fishers seem to take stonefly fishing very seriously, because when the stonefly hatch is good, it's very good, like a bonus for being so patient all winter; and when it's bad, we're not really surprised. Then, most fly fishers resort to drifting Stonefly Nymphs, hoping for some surface activity before they have to go home. I think most of us realize that nymphing will be the major activity of the day even before we leave home early in the morning armed with sandwiches and a Thermos of hot coffee—and maybe even a small backpack stove and coffeepot to brew some fresh coffee when the Thermos runs dry. They are long, bone-chilling, often fishless days. I call them "dues paying" days, which I'm expected to spend if I'm to have the faintest hope of hitting good mayfly hatches during the summer and fall.

Catching the salmon fly hatch can be either feast or famine, trout fishing at its very best—outstanding often enough to keep us going back every spring, even though the last time we really hit the hatch was four or five years ago.

Some fly tyers spend hours trying to tie a Stonefly Nymph that looks exactly like the natural—complete with the correct number of body segments, wing pads, gill filaments, tapered and bent legs meticulously painted with felt-tip pens, eyes, tails, and antennae—only to lose it on a rock on the first cast. The Stonefly Nymph must be fished on the bottom, and this usually means bouncing it over and between rocks specifically designed by nature to grab and hold a fly. If you are that kind of fly tyer and have that kind of luck, you can expect more frustration added to days that usually have a certain amount already built in.

The late Charlie Brooks was a master of simplicity when it came to tying flies. His Brooks's Stone Nymph is the epitome of unadorned effectiveness. I had the opportunity to discuss stonefly patterns with him at his home years ago, and he talked at length about what a waste of time he thought it was to spend all that time striving for an ultrarealistic stonefly imitation that would soon be lost among the rocks on the stream bottom. He went on to explain that the stonefly nymph crawls to the stream bank, where it attaches itself to a rock, a willow trunk (hence the name willow fly), or anything dry; the thorax then splits at the top, and the winged adult emerges, mates, lays eggs, and dies. The migration from midstream to bank is when the stonefly nymphs are most vulnerable because they often lose their grips on the rocks in the fast currents and drift downstream until they can gain footholds and continue their migration. The trout literally line up three or four feet from shore and wait for this. Charlie said, "Now, think about that. It's spring, snowmelt has often begun, the streams are beginning to get a little off-color, the trout probably feel safe being in shallow water that's cloudy, where all of a sudden there's lots of food. The nymphs are tumbling downstream and the trout will grab anything that's the right size. If it's a stick, they'll spit it out. If it's a bug, they'll eat it. My Stonefly Nymph looks right to the trout, no matter if the fly is right-side up or upside down. It looks like a stonefly nymph from any angle." He was absolutely right. Jack Dennis included the pattern in his very popular *Western Trout Fly Tying Manual*, Volume II.

My Stonefly Nymphs fall somewhere between Charlie Brook's simple patterns, and museum-quality masterpieces, leaning much closer to simplicity than to works of art. I want a fly that is a little more realistic, but still quick and easy to tie, so I won't go into tantrums when I lose it. I call it "A. K.'s Black Ugly Nymph," and use versions of it for golden and brown stones. My pattern is similar to many other Stonefly Nymph patterns, with a few modifications. First, I tie the flies very large. Measure the naturals, then decide. I also tie them without antennae. An entomologist told me that the stonefly nymph folds its antennae back over its body while drifting in the current; as soon as its legs touch a rock and the nymph gets a grip on things, its antennae spring forward. He illustrated this by catching a few and releasing them in the current; they did exactly what he'd described. I figure this is good to know, because it makes tying the Stonefly Nymph one step easier and faster, and also simplifies tying the fly to leader. I always seem to get one antenna tangled in the knot at the very moment I'm tightening it. And contrary to popular beliefs, the nymphs don't curl up when drifting. If they did, they

Black stonefly nymph

Black Ugly Nymph

couldn't use their legs to grab hold of any rocks they might bounce against. These are two more examples in a long list of assumptions we make about insects while we're holding them in our hand. Insects don't live in our hands, and that's not where trout eat them. We should ask, "How does the natural look in or on the water?" It only takes a few moments to make a few observations like this, and what you learn will always be valuable, both at the tying bench and on the stream.

NOTE: See chapter 18 for detailed tying instructions for this fly.

BLACK UGLY NYMPH

Hook:	Mustad 79580, #2 and #4
Thread:	Danville's Monocord #100 black.
Tail:	Pair of black-dyed goose biots, one on each side of the hook, length to equal hook-gap distance. Separate the biots with a tiny ball of black dubbing.
Underbody:	Lash a piece of lead wire (.030" or .035" diameter) to each side of the hook shank.
Ribbing:	3/32"-wide black Swannundaze.
Body:	Large (nearly ¼"-wide) black wool knitting yarn.
Wing Case:	A ¼"-wide segment of black-dyed goose secondary wing feather, or black-dyed wild turkey tail feather. Spray liberally with Krylon Workable Fixatif to prevent splitting.
Legs:	One black hen back feather, tied in on top of wing case quill.
Thorax:	Dirty orange Australian 'possum dubbing.

NOTE: Bend the completed nymph with your thumbs and forefingers to give the hook a reverse curve.

SALMON FLY ADULTS

I fished my first salmon fly hatch on Montana's Madison River in 1976 with Koke Winter. It was my first trip from my home in Michigan to fish the fabled waters of the West, and, as luck would have it, it was the year of the Mother of All Stonefly Hatches. Folks who were lucky enough to be there still talk about it. Just the mention of the Stonefly Hatch of '76 brings warm smiles and glazed eyes as we remember the perfect weather, the low stream level, the thousands of flies, and the ravenous trout. We had four or five thirty- to forty-fish days. All the trout were caught on dry flies and ranged to seven pounds. The low water made wading the Madison that spring as good as wading the Madison can get. (Those who wade the Madison know about the "knee deep" rule: If you are in over your knees, you'll soon be in over your waders and downstream a considerable distance. The Madison's strong currents can easily become life threatening.) It was one of those glorious events that happens only once or twice in a lifetime of fishing. Koke said later, "I suppose you think it's like this every year?" I said, "Isn't it?" He answered, "If you live to be a hundred, you'll probably never see this again." I'm not a hundred yet, but I keep looking. So far he's right.

The most popular pattern at the time was the Sofa Pillow—a dry-fly pattern of the adult salmon fly that doesn't float worth a damn. We'd catch one or two fish on a Sofa Pillow then change flies, because it wouldn't float anymore. The original pattern had a floss body and a gray squirrel tail wing, and double-hackle collar. Not much buoyancy there. I tried tying an underbody of elk overwrapped with orange yarn, with a gray elk wing and about four hackles in the collar. It was an improvement, but it didn't really resemble the natural very closely. On the second day of the hatch I watched what the naturals did on the water, and made some crude sketches on a matchbook cover. Here's what I noticed then, and still notice today:

1. The natural floats heavily on the water, about half in and half above the surface.

2. The legs are constantly in a running or swimming motion.

3. The wings are often in motion, but not usually fluttering violently.

4. The tails are not noticeable.

5. The leg placement covers the front half of the entire body.

6. The antennae are held above the water.

7. There is only a little orange at the thorax.

8. The abdomen is not fuzzy, but dull, smooth, and prominently segmented.

9. The naturals drop suddenly from the sky as if shot, and land on the water with a plop.

I don't see artificials in the fly shops that look like that. So, as you may have guessed, I have a pattern for the adult salmon fly that I think incorporates all the above traits. It isn't easy to tie, and that's a drawback. But, it floats heavily on the water without sinking, its soft rooster hackle provides some leg motion, and it's quite durable and very visible. I tied a half dozen of the following pattern for each of us on the second night of our stay at the Alpine Motel in West Yellowstone. The following day, Koke and I were into fish on what now seems like every other cast. We were so successful that other fishermen began asking us what fly we were using. Unfortunately for me, eight of Koke's friends from Denver were staying at the Alpine Motel with us, and I was up till 2 A.M. tying #2 Black Ugly Stonefly Adults for what seemed like the entire town. I was glad I did, because I have never since seen so many fishermen catch so many fish on flies I had tied. As a fly tyer, there is a great deal of satisfaction in that. This hasn't become a popular pattern because it's difficult to tie. There are lots of simplified versions on the market today by other tyers. That's fine with me, but they're still not *the* Black Ugly.

Black stonefly adult (photo by John Gierach)

Black Ugly Stonefly Adult

NOTE: See chapter 18 for detailed tying instructions for this fly.

BLACK UGLY STONEFLY ADULT

Hook: Mustad 79580, #6, #4, and #2.
Thread: Danville's Flat Waxed Nylon #100 black.

> *Tail:* None.
>
> *Body:* Clump of black-dyed elk body hair, diameter of a standard lead pencil.
>
> *Thorax:* Clump of orange-dyed elk body hair, diameter of a standard lead pencil.
>
> *Thorax Hackle:* Two black-dyed soft rooster neck butt hackles with lots of web.
>
> *Wings:* Clump of natural gray elk body hair, diameter of a standard lead pencil.
>
> *Hackle Collar:* Two black-dyed soft rooster neck butt hackles with lots of web.

GOLDEN STONES

I can more or less count on hitting the salmon fly hatch once out of four or five years, but the golden stone hatch has evaded me for at least the past ten. I carry a box of both throughout the spring, but usually end up fishing nymphs during the golden stone hatch. There never seem to be enough adults around to tempt the trout to the surface, but they'll gobble up nymphs all day long. Another nice thing about the Golden Stone Nymph is that it often takes trout throughout the year. I've resorted to a Golden Stone Nymph many times during those periods between mayfly hatches. It helps to keep some mental notes on where you've seen goldens in the past, because it usually means that the trout in that section of the stream are always on the lookout for a free-drifting stonefly nymph. The strike is often anything but subtle, as it is with tiny baetis nymphs or midge larvae. I don't count nymph fishing as a real fun thing to do, and have always considered it only slightly better than not fishing, but when I'm fishing Stonefly Nymphs things can get pretty exciting. Both golden stone and the salmon fly nymphs are bigger than most other foods in the stream, and bigger trout seem more interested in grabbing mouthfuls than in sucking in something microscopic. I've also noticed that larger trout seem to inhabit streams with good populations of stoneflies.

My Golden Stone Nymph pattern differs from my Salmon Fly Nymph only in hook size and color of materials.

Golden stone nymph

Golden Stone Nymph

NOTE: See chapter 18 for detailed tying instructions for this fly.

GOLDEN STONE NYMPH

Hook:	Mustad 79580, #8 and #6.
Thread:	Danville's monocord #8 yellow.
Tail:	Rooster pheasant wing biots.
Underbody:	Two pieces of .025" or .030" lead wire, lashed one on each side of the hook.
Ribbing:	Danville's Flat Waxed Nylon #8 yellow.
Shellback/ *Wingcase:*	Bronze wild turkey secondary wing feather segment.
Abdomen:	Golden yellow wool yarn or dubbing.
Legs:	Mottled tan hen back feather.
Thorax:	Same as abdomen.

GOLDEN STONE ADULTS

I use a simpler pattern for the golden stone adult than the salmon fly. Since it's smaller, I believe I can get by with less realism. When I have been lucky enough to hit the golden stone hatch, this pattern works very well. It also doubles nicely for some large caddis that I have come across on some lakes.

NOTE: See chapter 18 for detailed tying instructions for this fly.

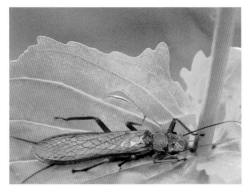 

Golden stone adult (photo by Dave Hughes)   *Golden Stone Adult*

GOLDEN STONE ADULT

Hook: Mustad 79580, #8 and #6.

Thread: Danville's monocord #8 yellow.

Underbody: A ³/₁₆"-clump of light natural elk body hair.

Overbody: Golden yellow wool yarn or dubbing.

Wings: A ³/₁₆"-clump of light natural elk body hair.

Hackle: Medium ginger dry-fly hackle.

BRONZE AND BROWN STONES

The midsized (size 8 to 10) bronze and brown stonefly hatches seem to occur when I'm occupied with early blue-winged olives. I've run across them in the late spring, in some streams in the Rockies, at elevations from 6,000 to 9,000 feet, but there are usually far more early season mayflies on the water than midsized stones. In my experience, the occasional trout will eat a bronze or brown stonefly, but most seem more interested in the mayfly hatch.

I don't carry many adult Bronze or Brown Stonefly patterns, because I have found that I can fish a size 6 or 8 Brown or Olive Fluttering Caddis with pretty fair success. I just haven't seen enough of these bugs on the waters I fish to be moved to come up with The Cosmic Pattern for them. The nymph pattern I use for bronze and brown stoneflies is the same as listed for the golden stone nymph, but with darker materials. In fact, a Hare's Ear Nymph (tied with a wing case) in size 6, 8, and 10 is an excellent imitation.

EARLY BROWN STONES

If you miss the salmon fly and golden stonefly hatches yet want to be able to say, "I fished a stonefly hatch this spring," have faith and keep visiting your stream on a weekly basis. When the little early brown stone hatch is in progress, you can count on some good fishing. Where I live in the West, the early brown stones come on just after the trees leaf out. The lower elevation snowmelt has ended, but the upper elevation snowmelt has yet to begin, so the streams at 5,000 to 6,000 feet are relatively clear and still safe to wade. The weather is simply glorious— migrating birds are everywhere, wildflowers and streamside bushes are in bloom, and it's pretty easy to get sunburned. In short, it's so damn good to be alive and out in the woods that you could easily forget to fish. If that sounds a little blasphemous, you haven't fished enough yet.

Like all hatches, the early brown stonefly hatch can range from just a few bugs here and there to thousands of insects that seem to fill the sky above the stream. They look a lot like caddis flies in flight, and I've seen people fish a dark olive or brown caddis dry with reasonably good success, but I believe you'll have greater success with a pattern that more accurately imitates the natural. I've photographed naturals from the top, side, and bottom, and made several (I think) important discoveries: The bodies are very shiny and reflect more light than most other insects; the leg placement covers at least the front half of the body; and the wings are a grayish brown color, but very translucent.

I have fooled around with a number of ideas for this pattern, and have settled on three versions, each intended for specific fishing conditions and insect activities. The first pattern, which is easy to tie with a hair wing, a dubbed body, and a palmered hackle, is for slightly overcast days, when most of the feeding activity seems to be in broken water. Fish this pattern with a slight twitch now and then. The second pattern has a shaped goose-segment wing, a very thinly dubbed body, and hackle collar, for when there are lots of spent stoneflies on the water. Fish it dead-drift from the middle to the tail of a pool. The third pattern has a quill body, a hackle collar, with a hackle fiber or mink-tail guard hair wing. Even though it's a little more difficult to tie, this is my favorite pattern, because it has more of the natural's physical characteristics. I also seem to catch more fish with it than the other patterns, but that could be because I fish more carefully when I'm using it. It works well in all water types and can be either twitched or dead drifted.

Early brown stone adult

Version 1.

Version 2.

Version 3.

NOTE: See chapter 18 for detailed tying instructions for the following patterns.

EARLY BROWN STONE 1

Hook: Mustad 94840 or Tiemco 100, #16 and #14.
Thread: Danville's 6/0 #100 black.
Body: Very fine chocolate brown dry-fly dubbing.

Hackle: Dark brown saddle or neck dry-fly hackle, palmer style. Clip the top fibers to allow for the hair wing.

Wings: Natural light gray deer body hair, slightly flared.

EARLY BROWN STONE 2

Hook: Mustad 94840 or Tiemco 100, #16 and #14.

Thread: Danville's 6/0 #100 black.

Body: Very fine chocolate brown dry-fly dubbing. Create a very thin body profile.

Wings: Segment of light gray goose wing, $5/32$" wide for #14 hook; $1/8$" wide for #16. The wing should extend one hook-gap distance beyond the hook bend.

Hackle: Dark dun saddle or neck hackle. The hackle collar should be sparse but cover ¼ of the front of the hook shank.

EARLY BROWN STONE 3

Hook: Mustad 94840 or Tiemco 100, #16 and #14.

Thread: Danville's 6/0 #100 black.

Body: One stripped and dark brown-dyed 7"-8" rooster neck hackle quill. Extend the body to within three hook-eye lengths of the eye.

Wings: Light medium dun spade hackle fibers or light medium dun-dyed mink-tail guard hairs. The wing should extend one hook-gap distance beyond the hook bend.

Hackle: Dark-dun hackle. The hackle collar should be sparse but cover the front quarter of the hook.

LITTLE YELLOW STONEFLIES

This delicate little pale yellow stonefly may well be the prettiest of all stoneflies. I don't usually associate good looks with stoneflies, because they are usually much larger, and even though they're absolutely harmless they have a certain aura of aggressiveness about them. They're big enough to bite off a serious chunk of meat from the back of your neck, if they could. Fortunately, they can't, but I've seen a lot of glasses ripped away from fisherman's faces as they frantically swiped at the bugs crawling up their necks.

The little yellow stonefly is a different matter. Seldom larger than a size 12, or maybe a 14 or 16, these delicate little flies seem less inclined to crawl behind your ears than the much larger salmon flies. Everything about them appears fragile, from their pale yellow color to their tiny black eyes. Body, legs, and wings all appear a little translucent, and sometimes I've noticed just a tinge of pale orange or pink on their prominently segmented and light-reflective bodies. I think the trout appreciate the beauty of these insects as must as we do, because they often take them with what I term a "respectful" rise. It's not the same aggressive splashy rise they make to the larger salmon flies, golden stones, and sometimes caddis flies, nor is it the leisurely sipping rise so often associated with small duns, midges, and spinners. If you can put your fly over a trout during the little yellow stonefly hatch, you'll probably catch him, provided your presentation is correct.

Some books list this as an eastern bug with no mention of the western hatch, some books list it as a western hatch with no mention of an eastern version. A couple of books are so highly technical that I can't determine which is which or where the bug exists. I do know that I have seen the little yellow stonefly from eastern waters to the Rocky Mountains, and have caught fish everywhere on the following pattern. Wherever you live, I'd be willing to bet you see the little yellow stonefly on your home waters.

Little yellow stonefly adult

Little Yellow Quill Stonefly

NOTE: See chapter 18 for detailed tying instructions for this fly.

LITTLE YELLOW QUILL STONEFLY

Hook: Mustad 94840 or Tiemco 100, #12, #14, #16.

Thread: Danville's 6/0 #8 yellow.

Body: One stripped and yellow-dyed 7"-8" rooster hackle quill.

Wings: One pale yellow dyed hen hackle tip.

Hackle: One pale yellow dyed dry-fly hackle feather.

SEVENTEEN

Terrestrials

If it weren't for ant, beetle, and hopper patterns, I would have more fish-less days than I'd care to admit. Ants are everywhere, crawling about on everything, including your waders. Sometimes you become painfully aware of their presence. Like the day John Gierach and I were standing on the bank of the South Platte River watching a large rainbow casually feeding on something against the far bank. We were so intent on watching the fish we didn't notice I was standing on a hill of fire ants. Hundreds of them swarmed up my waders, onto my neck and arms, and let me know with their burning stings that I was not welcome. It's amazing how fast you can get out of your vest, waders, and shirt while swiping at ants—without breaking your rod or glasses. The urgent call of nature is a comparatively casual event.

I know a few people who fish an ant pattern during a hatch of pale morning duns or blue-winged olives, and they often catch as many fish as us hatch-matchers with our realistic mayfly patterns. This can be disconcerting if you're really proud of your mayfly imitations.

Ants do crawl on everything—overhanging grass, bushes, rocks, trees—and in a slight breeze many lose their footing and fall. When the midsummer hatch doldrums set in, you'd better have some ant patterns with you. It's a time when trout don't show themselves as often as they do during the regular hatch of mayflies or caddis flies. It's a time when you can get to know your favorite stream a little better, because if you're going to have any luck, you're going to have to fish the water. Cast the fly to the most likely places a trout could be holding: an undercut bank, next to a log, in front of a rock, the current creases on either side of a rock or the dead water immediately behind it, or at the very lip of the tail of a large or small pool. At this time of year you must make the effort to see beyond the stream's surface. If there is something on the bottom big enough to noticeably disturb the surface, you can bet some serious money there will be a trout there, even if you can't see it. Trout survive by *not* being seen.

I don't have an ant pattern that's any better than any other ant pattern you may have seen. But I do have a couple hints on the tying of a dubbed-body ant pattern (which I prefer) that will make your fly look a lot more like an ant to you—and probably to the trout as well.

Red Ant

Black Ant

NOTE: See chapter 18 for detailed tying instructions for this fly.

BLACK OR RED ANT

Hook: Mustad 94840 or Tiemco 100 for size 16. Mustad 94842 or Tiemco 101 for size 18 and smaller.

Thread: Danville's 6/0 #100 black, or #429 tan; or Uni-Thread 8/0 black or camel.

Body: Black-dyed beaver (Black Ant). Dyed or blended cream-tan-rust beaver (Red Ant).

Hackle: One black hackle, four to five turns for Black Ant. One medium brown hackle, four to five turns for Red Ant.

Head: Same dubbing as body.

FLYING ANTS

As long as you're tying ants, you may as well tie a few of the flying variety, because you're going to need them. When spring comes, put the ant box in your vest and leave it there. I generally know about when to expect flying ants on most of my favorite streams, although like all things having to do with nature, they'll show up when they're ready; when the trout key in on them, flying ants may be the exclusive food of the day, whether there's a mayfly hatch on or not. Be prepared.

I normally tie Flying Ants one size larger than regular ants. A size-14 Red or Black Flying Ant may sound too big, but I've fished that size a lot more than a size 16 or 18.

NOTE: See chapter 18 for detailed tying instructions.

Red flying ant

Red Flying Ant

Black Flying Ant

THE MYSTERY FLY

I remember reading about this little insect years ago in one of the trout fishing magazines. I think I remember it as some sort of aquatic insect, but it looks so much like a terrestrial that I'm going to include it here. Most folks call it a "black midge," which it isn't; others call it a "black flying ant," which it also isn't. I can't remember the name of this insect, or the author of the article, or even which magazine the article was in. But I vividly remember all the late evenings John Gierach and I spent on a favorite stretch of the St. Vrain River marveling at how many trout were rising, wondering where they all came from, and trying to determine what they were eating. At times there were large size-14 and -16 chocolate spinners on the water, and we wore out more than a few imitations casting to all those rising trout, without success. At other times we could see nothing on the water, yet trout were rising everywhere. We'd walk back to the truck long after dark, mumbling about the Mystery Hatch. Finally we were able to net a few tiny, size-22 and -24 black insects that looked more like fleas than flies, but we doubted they could be the cause of all that feeding activity. We did fish size-22 Black Midges and caught a few small browns, but so few that we figured the midge wasn't the real answer for the Mystery Hatch, which begins mid- to late summer and lasts for many weeks.

I made a point one evening two years ago to stop fishing and net a few of the insects, to sketch them and to take some notes about their body shapes, lengths, and other details, since it was far too dark for photos. I found that the insect was definitely not a midge, because the body was too fat; and the clear white wings were upright but not divided, which also meant it couldn't be a flying ant. Size 24 was a good match for length, but I tied some 22s as well. John was off to Alaska on a book-signing tour by then, and I hoped to discover the answer to the Mystery Hatch while he was gone.

I tried my new pattern and it worked—to the tune of nearly two dozen fish landed, with a half-dozen flies lost on a 7X tippet. When John got back and reported on the dozens of big salmon, char, and steelhead he'd caught in Alaska, I said, "O.K., are you ready for a reality check?" and told him about the new pattern. We were on the St. Vrain the following evening, the little Mystery Fly worked its magic, and we caught and released dozens of fish. One of the pure joys of being a fly tyer is coming up with a pattern that solves a seemingly impossible situation, and watching your best friend catch fish with it.

Mystery fly

Mystery Fly

NOTE: See chapter 18 for detailed tying instructions for this fly.

MYSTERY FLY

    Hook: Mustad 94842 or Tiemco 101, #24 and #22.

  Thread: Uni-Thread 8/0 black.

    Body: Very fine black dubbing (beaver is excellent). Create a thin, cigar-shaped body.

   Wings: Pair of white hen hackle tips, length to equal entire hook. Tie in as you would dun wings, but do not stand them up or divide them.

  Hackle: One black dry-fly hackle, tied collar style.

When fishing this fly, don't be dismayed if it doesn't land upright. Some of the naturals look like spinners and lie flat on the water, but most have fallen over to one side. The rise form is very subtle. The bugs are on the water from late dusk until well into nightfall; look for them in the slow, flat water of any large pool.

BEETLES

At times in late summer, even ants won't bring up a trout no matter how well your fly is tied or presented. You begin to wonder if trout take afternoon naps, and maybe you think it would be a good idea to climb out of the stream and take one yourself. You should try a beetle first. I've always carried a few beetles in my fly box, because I sometimes run into a fisherman who is catching an occasional trout while no one else is having any luck. When asked the obvious, "What're you using?," the reply is often "beetle." When followed with "What size and color?," the answer is usually some form of "black or brown, size 16, 18, or 20." I always hesitate to ask any more questions, because I figure the guy came out to fish, not to be interviewed. So I tie on a small beetle and almost always catch a fish or two. It's a dependable fly of last resort.

The main trouble with beetle patterns is durability. To get them to float, most patterns rely on dyed elk or deer hair to imitate the hump-shaped shellback of the natural. The problem is, catching one or two trout inevitably destroys the fly. I think this is why most of us hesitate to use beetle patterns very often. Why spend a lot of time tying a very realistic beetle pattern only to have some 7-inch trout tear it all to hell the first time you use it? If you're not going to fish it, then why tie it? You might as well take a nap!

There is a solution to the beetle durability problem called "Bugskin"—a very thin, smooth, shaved leather sheet that is a byproduct of leather-goods production. Bugskin was discovered by Chuck Furimsky, who operates a leather-goods shop in Seven Springs Mountain Resort in Pennsylvania. Chuck is a fly tyer and fly fisherman, and always on the lookout for something he can use to tie more realistic and durable flies. His crayfish and aquatic worm patterns using Bugskin are the best I have ever seen.

Bugskin is available in a variety of colors, including such beetlelike metallic finishes as bronze, peacock, and silver-black. Need I say more? It's also incredibly durable, and will float all day after being impregnated with a good paste silicone flotant. I took six browns on the first size-18 Bronze Beetle I tied with Bugskin, and it floated as well after the sixth fish at it did on the first cast, and retained its shape. Bugskin is marketed by Phil Camera of Inter-Tac (PO Box 6340, Woodland Park, CO 80866). I seldom promote a product, out of fairness to other suppliers, but this new product is so outstanding I simply can't remain quiet about it.

Bugskin Beetle, Bronze

Bugskin Beetle, Black

NOTE: See chapter 18 for detailed tying instructions for the following patterns.

BUGSKIN BEETLE, BRONZE

Hook:	Mustad 94840 or Tiemco 100, #22, #20, #18, #16.
Thread:	Danville's 6/0 #100 black, or Uni-Thread 8/0 black.
Shellback:	Strip of bronze or peacock Bugskin.
Body:	Very fine brown dubbing (beaver or rabbit).
Hackle:	Palmered body, with brown hackle.

BUGSKIN BEETLE, BLACK

Hook:	Mustad 94840 or Tiemco 100, #18, #16, #14.
Thread:	Danville's #100 black, or Uni-Thread 8/0 black.
Shellback:	Strip of black, or metallized gold, silver, or peacock black Bugskin.
Body:	Peacock herl, or fine black dubbing.
Hackle:	Palmered body, with black hackle.

NOTE: If you use peacock herl for the body, expect the fly to float about two inches beneath the surface. If you want the Black Beetle to float on the surface, use black dubbing instead.

This can be a deadly pattern if you don't happen to have the correct mayfly emerger! There are many other colors of Bugskin available to imitate the beetles common to your area. I have found that Bronze and Black Beetles in several sizes are all I need.

HOPPERS

Everyone I know who fly fishes carries two or three hopper patterns. Most are quite small, ranging from a size 14 to no more than a 10. I lean toward the thought that hoppers are big and get bigger, and tie most of mine in sizes 6, 8, and 10. If the naturals are smaller than that, I fish a little yellow or light olive St. Vrain Caddis.

I also tie my hoppers in three different colors. I started doing this years ago, after fishing a high altitude meadow stream on a windy day. The surrounding hay fields and pastureland were heavily infested with grasshoppers, and my fishing partner and I watched the trout eat every one that got blown in. Naturally, we tied on hopper patterns of the appropriate size, but we caught only a few fish. We did a little hopper catching and discovered that they all had pale green bodies. We were using the standard yellow wool yarn. This was the first time I had experienced color preference with hopper patterns. So I tied a half-dozen hoppers with pale green bodies and returned to the stream about a week later. If you think I'm going to say, "and they worked just fine," you're absolutely right. They worked so well that now I'm never without the green version in several sizes; I like them to be a bit smaller than the yellow pattern—size 8 to 12.

Judging from the fly bins of most fly shops, someone or a group of someones has evidently decided that all hoppers are yellow. I know there are a few folks who fish a size-18 Royal Wulff when a size-18 pale morning dun hatch is on. I always figured these folks were more interested in casting than catching. Fishing a Yellow Hopper when the green guys are out makes about as much sense as fishing a Royal Wulff during a PMD hatch.

In addition to the standard yellow and the smaller green hopper, there is what I call the plains hopper, or tan hopper. I usually find it at around five thousand feet in elevation and lower. These dirty grayish tan hoppers are the ones you can hear before you see when they're flying, and they get quite big. I tie them on #8, #6, and #4 hooks, and when I fish them I try to cause as much commotion as possible without spooking the fish. The naturals are pretty good fliers and don't often get in the stream, but when they do, it's a crash landing that seems to trigger a reflex rise from the trout. Use a strong tippet!

I have tied and fished the Joe's Hopper, the Letort Hopper, and the Whitlock Hopper, and have caught fish on them all. But I have also had lots of refusals, even when I used the right size and color. All three are standard patterns and very popular nationally. Most fly shops sell these three patterns, and two or three others that are similar in profile. It occurred to me that a yellow hopper is a yellow hopper, period. Why, then, do we have a half-dozen or more patterns? Maybe it's because other tyers have seen situations where the trout were feeding on yellow hoppers but wouldn't eat their artificials. That's how new fly patterns are born.

Each pattern mentioned above has a characteristic or feature that I think makes it outstanding. The Joe's Hopper has a nice, fat wool-yarn body, with a short trailing loop as a body extension, and a palmer-hackled body, which give it a nice buggy appearance. The wing is bad, though, because it is usually wrapped too low around each side of the body. Its profile isn't nearly as good as that of the Letort Hopper's wing, which is flatter and a lot easier to tie. And I like the idea of using a little deer hair over the top of the wing quill segment, to give the appearance of legs, or perhaps of a slight fluttering action from the struggling insect. The body of the Letort Hopper looks a little too clean, however. The only hopper with a decent head shape is Dave Whitlock's pattern. So I borrowed what I think is the most important feature of each pattern, and created A. K.'s Hopper. It has a Joe's Hopper body, a Letort Hopper wing, and a Whitlock-style clipped deer hair head. The combination of patterns produces a hopper that floats heavily in the water like the natural, yet it won't sink, and it's highly visible. Use the same pattern recipe for all three colors.

Yellow Hopper

Green Hopper

Tan Hopper

NOTE: See chapter 18 for detailed tying instructions for this pattern.

A. K.'S HOPPER

Hook:	Mustad 94831, #12, #10, #8, #6.
Thread:	Danville's Prewaxed Monocord: #8 yellow for the Yellow Hopper; #60 light green for the Green Hopper; #41 tan for the Tan Hopper.
Body:	Four-strand Orlon or wool yarn, yellow, pale green, or tan.
Hackle:	Brown, palmer style, for all three patterns.
Underwing:	Mottled brown wild turkey wing feather segment.
Overwing:	Small clump of elk body or deer body hair.
Head:	Spun and trimmed deer hair.

EIGHTEEN

Tying Instructions

QUILL-BODIED DUNS

1. Start the tying thread at the middle of the hook shank, and wrap tight turns back to the *beginning* of the hook bend. Clip off the tag end of the tying thread before you get to the bend, to prevent a tiny tuft of clipped thread from appearing later under the tailing fibers. Take one extra turn of thread over the last turn, to form a tiny thread bump. This will cock the tailing fibers slightly upward, to more accurately imitate the natural's tail position.

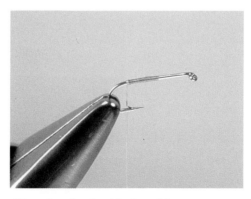

Thread on hook with thread bump

TAILING

2. Clip off seven to ten stiff spade hackle fibers, measure them to be one hook-eye length longer than the entire hook, from the leading edge of the eye to the trailing edge of the bend. Use this length for all sizes, unless the natural has a longer or shorter tail. Use four to six spade fibers for #20 and smaller, and seven to ten fibers for #18 and larger.

3. Grasp the tips with your left thumb and forefinger and lay the fibers against the side of the hook facing you at about a 45-degree angle, with the butts below the hook shank. Take one loose turn of thread around the hook shank and the fibers, and tighten the thread with a quick downward motion on the bobbin tube. Thread torque should begin to move the hackle fibers around toward the top of the hook shank. As you bring the tying thread up around the hook shank for the second turn of thread, be careful that it goes in front of the first turn, and allow it to continue pushing the hackle fibers toward the top of the shank. All the tailing fibers should be on top of the shank after completing the third turn of thread. Continue to pull up on the tips of the tailing fibers as you wrap the thread toward the eye. Clip off the tailing butts at a point about three hook-eye lengths behind the eye, and stop the thread wraps at this point.

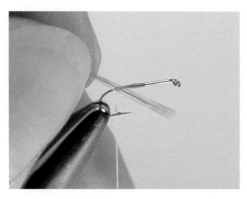

Tailing in place

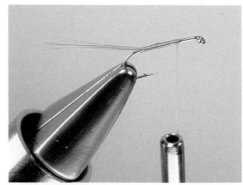

Tailing tied in

BODY

4. For #16 and larger hooks, select two quills, one about a third smaller in diameter than the other. Clip off the tips at a point where their combined width is equal to the diameter of the hook shank and the tailing fibers. For #18 and smaller hooks, use only one quill. Tie in the clipped tips exactly over the clipped tailing butts, and spiral-wrap tying thread toward the rear of the hook and back again to a point three hook-eye lengths behind the eye. Refer to the practice exercises in chapter 1. Be very careful to not create any thread bumps as you tie in the quills.

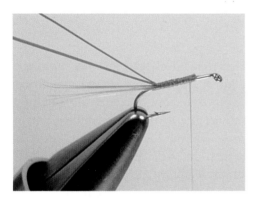

Two quills tied in

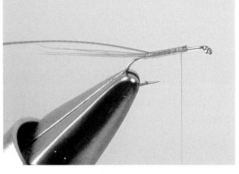

One quill tied in

5. Pull the quills straight away from you and begin wrapping them forward toward the eye. If tying with two quills, the thinner quill should be in front of the thicker one, so that it becomes the leader and the thicker quill becomes the follower and covers the thinner. Be sure that the thicker quill covers the last wrap of thread anchoring your tailing material as you bring it around on the first turn. Whether you are tying with one or two quills, there should be no gaps between successive turns as you wrap them forward. Tie off and clip the quill butts at the same point as the tailing fibers. I like to refer to this position as the *point of winging*.

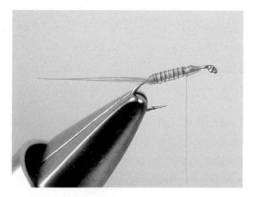

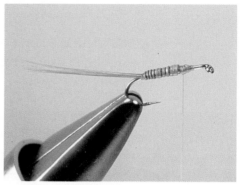

Finished two-quill body   *Finished one-quill body*

WINGS

6. Select a pair of medium dun pullet neck feathers with   as much
    web as possible. The width of the feathers should match the
    width of the hook gap for any hook size. Measure for length by
    aligning the tips of the feathers one hook-eye length longer than
    the length of the entire hook. Transfer the grip to your left hand
    without moving the feathers, and clip them off so that the
    clipped butts are even with the leading edge of the hook eye. You
    should now have a pair of hackle tips that are exactly one hook-
    eye length longer than the entire hook. If you use one hook-eye
    length of the butts for tie-down space, you will usually end up
    with wings of the correct length for most species of mayflies.

7. Hold the wings by their tips and place them on the hook, butts
    forward toward the eye, straddling the hook shank at an angle of
    about 45 degrees, and lean them toward you at about a 45-
    degree angle. Take one loose turn of thread around the butts and
    quickly tighten the thread with a sudden downward tug of the
    bobbin tube. Continue wrapping the thread around the shank
    for a second turn over the wing butts; as you wrap, pull the butts
    from under the thread just enough to see some movement, and
    lean them upright toward the top of the hook shank. This is the
    only way you can get the clipped butts exactly on top of the hook
    shank for later separation. Take two or three more turns of
    thread to anchor the wings.

Wings tied in

8. Separate the wings by placing the fingernail of your left index finger immediately behind and against the base of the wings, and push forward with a slight, rolling motion. The wings should pop apart in a nearly perfect V-shaped separation. Bring the tying thread up in front of the wings, then take one thread wrap between and down behind the far wing. Pull forward on the thread until you see the wing move into place, then take one complete turn of thread around the hook in front of both wings to lock it in place. Now bring the thread up behind the wing nearest you, then forward between the wings, and pull forward to align this wing with the first. When you're satisfied they're perfectly positioned, take one thread wrap around the hook in front of both wings to lock them in place. Leave the thread hanging in front of the wings.

Wings in place

HACKLE

9. Select a medium dun hackle, trim the butt, and tie the trimmed
   butt in front of the wings so that the tip of the hackle feather is
   toward the rear of the fly and between the wings. Don't wrap the
   butt of the hackle with thread all the way to the wings; save just
   enough space to begin winding the hackle by pulling the hackle
   straight away from you and down without disturbing the placement of the far wing. Continue wrapping the hackle by coming
   around underneath the body of the fly and up immediately
   behind the wings. Take two or three turns of hackle behind the
   wings, then bring the hackle forward under the wings and continue wrapping it until you run out of either hackle or space to
   put it. Clip off the tip and whip-finish. It makes no difference
   which side of the hackle is facing you; you want a bushy-looking
   hackle, with some fibers extending toward the bend and some
   extending beyond the eye—just like the natural's legs. This
   bushy hackle will support your fly a lot better than the traditional, tight vertical hackle collar, since more hackle points will
   be in contact with the water.

Hackle tied in   *Hackle wrapped*

For more complete details for tying this and other patterns, consult
my book *Production Fly Tying* (Pruett Publishing, Boulder, CO, 1989).

PARACHUTES

Ask six people why a parachute seems so much more effective than a dun on certain days and you'll probably get six different answers, ranging from "I can see the fly better," to "I think it represents the emerger." I think all the theories I've ever heard are correct to some degree. Parachutes are so effective that I'm never without a boxful of a wide variety of sizes and patterns. I often use a parachute at the beginning of a hatch and then again at the end, just as the spinners are beginning to come down. It's also great for prospecting in the evening when the light is fading fast, there are no bugs on the water and no rises to be seen, and I still feel like fishing and want to cast a fly I can see on the water. This has resulted in some significant fish-catching when most other anglers are back at their trucks putting their gear away. It is also some of the most pleasant angling of the year, simply because it's one of the few times I can really enjoy some pure solitude.

The parachute as traditionally tied, using either white calftail or white calf body hair for the wing, has its problems. A wing that is long and dense enough to both represent the natural insect's wing and be seen by the fisherman is so heavy that the fly tends to land on its side. This might present an interesting view to the fish, but it makes the fly impossible for the angler to see, especially after dusk. White or yellow poly yarn is a good substitute for the calf hair, but it's not that easy to work with, and makes a big bump where it's tied in; plus, for some reasons I don't really understand, I just plain don't like the looks of the finished fly. Maybe it's because yarn seems to poof out too much, looking more like a weed seed on the water than a fly.

Then I discovered white turkey T-base feathers, which grow on the necks and breasts of white turkeys. These feathers are only 2 to 4 inches long. Don't confuse them with turkey flats, which grow on the backs of birds, are about 5 to 8 inches long, and are not suitable for parachute wings because the ends of the feather fibers are too thin and filmy looking, and the feathers are too soft. I was experimenting with dyed and sprayed turkey T-base feathers (instead of rooster pheasant back) in an effort to come up with a permit crab fly that didn't take half a day to tie. I noticed that the fibers of the turkey T-base feathers adhered to each other, and that all the fiber tips were perfectly aligned—even after a segment had been clipped from the feather. When tied firmly to the hook,

T-base feather segments compress very nicely with fewer wraps of thread than calf hair; there is also no unsightly oversized bump where the wing post is tied in. Not only that, but once the post is treated with a drop of head lacquer and then wrapped at the base with tying thread, it's stiff enough to wrap a hackle around without holding! It's lighter in weight than calf hair, which means I can use more of it without creating a top-heavy fly, and it is extremely durable. Most fly shops have it, though it's often mislabeled. Ask for the two- to four-inch feathers.

QUILL-BODIED PARACHUTE

These instructions should be followed for any quill-bodied parachute, of any size.

1. Start the thread on the hook as described in the instructions for tying the Quill-bodied dun, above.

TAILING

2. The parachute body will always be on the water, not above it, as can happen with the standard dun pattern. Thus, stiffer, slightly denser, and longer tailing is needed to support the heaviest part of the hook, the bend. Tie in two or three more spade hackle fibers than you would use for a comparably sized dun pattern. They should also be at least one to two hook-eye lengths longer.

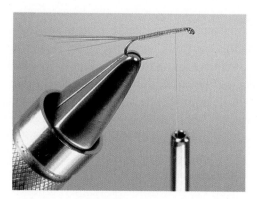

Parachute tailing tied in

Clip off the butts at a point two hook-eye lengths behind the eye, leaving just enough space behind the eye for the hackle tie-in, tie-off, and whip-finish. Bring the thread all the way to the eye and back to where you clipped off the tailing butts.

WING POST

3. Select a good, dense white turkey T-base feather, with a clean, sharp tip edge. Strip away all the marabou-like fibers until the tip of the feather is straight across to the center quill.

Stripped white turkey T-base feather

4. Holding the feather by its tip, clip a segment about ¼ inch wide for #16 hooks, slightly less than ¼ inch for #18, and corre-

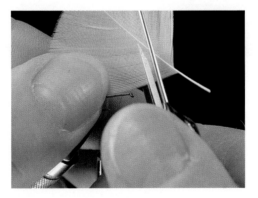

Clipping segment from feather

spondingly narrower for each smaller size. Make the cut at a 90-degree angle to the grain of the feather fibers. Hold the tip of the segment firmly between your left thumb and forefinger, and pull the remainder of the feather away.

5. Fold or roll the segment to form a wing post, being careful to keep the tips perfectly aligned. The more you handle the segment, the more fibers want to migrate out of alignment.

6. Hold the segment by its butt end and place it against your side of the shank, with the tips pointing down below the hook at a 45-degree angle, tips toward the eye. Take one loose turn of thread around the segment and the hook shank, and give the thread a quick tug straight down with the bobbin tube. Continue with a second turn of thread, using thread to push the tips up and around to the top of the hook. Check now to be certain that you have the wing post positioned exactly where you want it. Then, continue wrapping the thread toward the rear of the hook, taking about five to six additional very tight wraps.

Holding segment in place   *Wing post tied on and ready for trimming butt*

7. Lift the wing post butts, place your scissors flat on top of the hook shank, and clip off the butts. This creates an angled cut that is easier to cover with thread. Cover the clipped butts with thread, forming a smooth taper to the wing post. Bring the thread forward of the wing post, lift the tips, and wrap seven or eight turns of thread tightly against the front of the wing post to form a

"thread dam," which will help hold the wing post upright. Put a small drop of head lacquer at the base of the wing post.

Wing post ready for wrapping

8. Bring the tying thread up and behind the wing post and make one complete turn of thread around its base, as close as possible to the top of the hook shank. Holding the tips of the wing post between your left thumb and forefinger, pull the tying thread straight *away* from you, with enough force that you'll be afraid the thread will break; this will gather all the wing post fibers into a very dense clump. Continue wrapping the wing post upward for about an ¹/₈ inch (you won't need to hold the post), using a little less thread tension on each successive wrap. Wind the thread back down the post and position it immediately to the rear of the clipped butts.

Wrapped wing post

BODY

9. Measure one or two quills (depending on hook size) for diameter, as described in the instructions for tying the dun. Tie in the clipped tips immediately behind the clipped and wrapped wing post butt. This will fill in the small bump created by the wing post butt and make wrapping the quill over it a lot easier, allowing you to create a smoothly tapered body right up to the base of the wing post. Wrap the quills as described in the dun instructions, and bring the tying thread forward to hang down in front of the wing post.

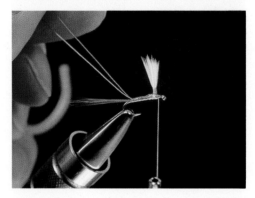

Quills tied in

10. Wrap the quills forward as in the dun instructions. When you get to the wing post, bring them up underneath and toward the

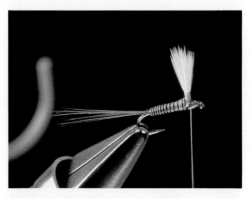

Completed quill body

front of the post; tie them down and clip them off in front of the post, on your side of the hook. Be very careful to cover the clipped butts completely with thread. Any tiny portion of clipped quill not covered with thread will surely reach out and grab the hackle tip, as you wind it around the wing post, and break it off.

HACKLE

11. Select a very stiff hackle—with absolutely no web—one size larger than you would normally use for your hook size (size-14 hackle for a #16 hook). Holding the hackle shiny-side up, clip three hook-eye lengths of fibers from the right side of the hackle, but only one hook-eye length of fibers from the left side. This is to ensure a clean hackle stem on the first turn around the wing post, which will help prevent it from twisting. Tie the clipped butt on your side of the hook immediately in front of the wing post so that the hackle tip points toward the rear of the fly at a 45-degree angle above the hook shank. Bring the thread back to hang down *immediately* in front of the wing post.

Parachute hackle tied in

12. Tying in the hackle for a parachute in the manner described in step 11 sets up the angle of the hackle feather so that the first turn of hackle around the wing post will be the top turn, and each successive turn of hackle will be below the first. Each turn

of hackle pulls down on the top turn, which helps prevent the hackle collar from sliding up the wing post. Take only four or five turns of hackle around the wing post and tie off the tip on your side of the hook, immediately in front of the wing post. Whip-finish, put a small drop of head lacquer on the head, and, at the top hackle wrap on the wing post.

For more details on tying the quill-bodied parachute, check the instructions for tailing, wing post, body, and hackling parachutes in *Production Fly Tying*.

SPINNERS

I've met a few people who hate to fish spinners. They complain that spinners are difficult to see, and they're right. But not fishing spinners is a certain way to ensure you'll catch fewer fish. The secret is getting close. I've discovered that, in the failing light of evening, when spinners are usually fished, I can get to within ten to twelve feet of a feeding fish without spooking it by very slowly working my way upstream to a point where I'm standing at about a 30-degree angle to the side of and above the fish. At a distance of ten to twelve feet, the spinner's white wings are easily visible and I can see the fish's very subtle take. I can also see the refusal rises, which often means I need a change in fly size.

Many people try to fish the spinner fall from a distance of twenty to thirty feet, as they have been fishing duns all day. It's amazing how close you can get to a steadily rising fish without spooking it if you're *very* careful in your approach. Whenever possible, I try to hide my silhouette against the streamside bushes and trees. And I don't wear light-colored shirts or hats at any time. I've never understood why a person would wear a white T-shirt or a baseball hat with a screaming yellow top on the stream. It's the first thing a trout sees.

If you find some rising trout on the far side of a large river and can't get close enough to them to see your spinner pattern on the water, try your pattern on some little dumb fish nearby. If they will eat it, chances are it's the same fly the big guys on the far side are feeding on. In that case, *you* don't need to see your fly; a trout will show you exactly where it is when he eats it!

When the season is well underway, it often can be very effective to begin your fishing day (if no hatch is on) by tying on a size 18 or 20 Red Quill or Rusty Quill Spinner, and fishing the slack-water spots along the edges of the stream and at the tails of the pools. Trout lying in these places are always looking up, and will at least give you the thrill of coming up to look at your fly. It's better than sitting on the bank.

Up to the last few years, most spinner patterns have had dubbed bodies. Even though the comparatively small diameter of a spinner's body is common knowledge, these dubbed-body flies are nearly always too fat, especially those tied in some foreign country, where the tyer has probably never *seen* a mayfly. Most of the dubbing on these flies is synthetic, which is highly touted for its floating qualities, but usually too spongy, and—in the small diameters needed to simulate the natural— almost impossible to dub into a neat, smooth, carrot-shaped body. Nearly all imported spinners have bodies identical in shape to the dun! It's a minor detail, but when you consider where a spinner is usually fished—glassy smooth, gin-clear water, where a trout can take all the time it wants to inspect your fly—silhouette and size become very important, more important than color.

A single quill is the closest thing to a perfect representation of the spinner body I've discovered. Body segmentation is represented, as are the waxy, light-reflecting qualities of the natural. And since the quill is about 90 percent air, trapped in thousands of tiny cells contained in the natural, enamel-like shell, its floating qualities are astoundingly good.

Spinner fishing often can be the most exciting fishing of the day, simply because you can never estimate the size of the fish rising to spinners. That tiny, dimplelike surface disturbance could be a ten-incher, or just as easily a twenty-incher. As the sun goes down and dusk comes over the stream, the bigger fish seem to lose a little of their caution. This is also the time when a lot of people leave the stream, either because they're afraid of the dark, or because they can't see the fly. Good for them! I love it then; more rising fish that I can get close to, and fewer fishermen! Isn't that what we want?

QUILL-BODIED SPINNER

1. Start the tying thread on the hook exactly as described for tying the dun.

TAILING

2. Select very stiff spade hackle fibers and tie them in as for the dun. I like to use a few less tailing fibers on spinners, because the natural is so sparse looking on the water. Measure them to be one or two hook-eye lengths longer than for the parachute or dun pattern. Wrap the tailing fibers forward and clip off the butts two hook-eye lengths behind the eye. We aren't concerned about saving space for a hackle collar, so we can set the wings nearer the eye.

BODY

3. Size, clip, and tie in one quill, as described for the dun, except tie in the end of the clipped quill tip two hook-eye lengths behind the eye.

4. Wrap the quill forward, tie it off, and clip off its butt two hook-eye lengths behind the eye.

5. Select a pair of white hen hackles whose width is one hook-eye length wider than the gap of the hook, and measure them to be two hook-eye lengths longer than the entire hook. In my experience, the wings of spinners are a little longer and wider than those of the same fly's dun. I prefer white hen hackles for spinner wings, because they become slightly translucent when treated with flotant, and they maintain their shape better than anything else I have tried.

6. Tie in the wings exactly as dun wings are tied in. However, when you separate them with your fingernail, continue to push forward and down until each wing is flat and perpendicular to the shank. Remember that you are setting the wings closer to the eye; it's the same position as the wing post on the parachute.

7. Figure-eight with tying thread as described for the dun. Bring the thread back to hang down immediately behind the wings.

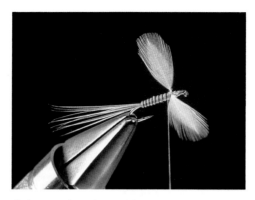

Spinner wings in position

Place a tiny drop of head lacquer on the hook shank at the base of the wings to help them maintain their position.

THORAX

8. Dub a very small amount of very fine dubbing on the thread, and take three to four turns immediately behind the wings to create a damming wall of dubbing immediately behind the wings; this will further ensure that the wings maintain their position. Then begin to figure-eight the dubbing around the wings, until you have built up a thorax at least two to three times the diameter of the quill body. It is important to add only very small amounts of dubbing to the thread; the dubbing rope should be just slightly thicker than the thread. If it becomes too thick, it will

Completed spinner

tend to roll over previous wraps of dubbing and destroy the wing position. When you finish, you should have just enough room behind the eye for the thread head and whip-finish.

If visibility is a problem for you when fishing spinners, simply tie in a hackle behind the wings before you dub the thorax, then dub the thorax and wind the hackle tightly in palmer fashion over the thorax, both behind and in front of the wings, and tie it off in front of the wings. Three or four turns of hackle is all you need. Clip off all the hackle from the bottom of the fly. The remaining hackle collar makes the fly quite visible, aids in floatation, and I believe adds to the effectiveness of the fly, since spinners *do* have legs.

Hackled spinner

NQ SPINNER

"NQ" means "Not Quite a Spinner." This stage in the life of some BWOs fooled me for more years than I care to admit. I vividly remember casting size 20, 22, and even 24 Olive Quill Duns to rising fish for hours without a single refusal rise. I'd stop fishing, net the water I was standing in, compare my little dun to those on the water, and continue to cast and cast and cast, changing fly sizes dozens of times. Parachutes, emergers, duns, spinners—nothing worked. But I could see dozens of tiny sailboat duns coming downstream only twenty feet away, the trout were actively feeding on them, and my little Olive Quill Duns were perfect matches for the bugs I had just netted. I changed tippets from 5X to 6X, from 6X to 7X, and finally extended the 7X length to thirty-six inches. Still no fish.

One evening two years ago, in a state of total exasperation, I decided to wade over into the feeding lane, spook all the trout, and net the water to find out what the hell they were eating. I didn't even have to net the water! As soon as I got into the current of *their* feeding lane, I could see the difference. They were eating spinners all right, but spinners that looked like duns from where I had been standing, because the insects' wings were still upright! The bodies were the same color as Red Quill Spinners, and the wings were clear like spinners', but those wings were still up and slightly divided—just like duns'. There were even some traditional spinners on the water, but the trout had decided they wanted the upright-winged versions, and they would have nothing to do with anything else. It was a classic case of a multiple hatch and multiple life-cycle stage, with a twist. I had been standing in a current that was delivering duns. The trout were lying in a current that was delivering spinners. I learned once again, never make assumptions.

Naturally, I tied up a dozen NQ Spinners the next morning in three different sizes, and was back on the stream the next day to find out if they would work. They did, and I now carry at least a dozen NQ Spinners, in sizes 18, 20, and 22, every time I go fishing. And, I'm happy to report, they work on many streams, not just the South Platte River in Colorado where I made this discovery. This is definitely a pattern worth carrying throughout the summer.

1. Tie the NQ Spinner exactly as you would the Quill-bodied Dun. The only differences are the tail and wing lengths should be those of spinner patterns, and that the body should be tied with only one quill, for any hook size.

WOUND-HACKLE SPINNER WINGS

Tie in the tail and quill body exactly as described in steps 1 through 4 for the Quill-bodied Spinner. When you get to step 5, follow the steps on page 136.

5. Select one spade hackle feather (*no* web!) two hackle sizes larger than your hook (#16 hook, size 12 hackle). With some hook sizes you may have to adjust the hackle size up or down, depending on the wing size of the insect you are attempting to imitate.

6. Clip and trim the hackle butt as in preparing any other hackle feather, and tie in the butt of the hackle immediately in front of the shoulder of the quill body.

7. Wrap the hackle very tightly for no more than five turns. "Tightly" means don't use up much hook shank space; you will need to save space for the dubbed thorax and head.

8. Tie down the hackle tip and clip it off. Bring the tying thread to a point immediately behind the hackle collar.

Hackle collar for spinner wings

9. Separate the hackle into two wings by placing your right thumb on top of the hackle collar and pushing down while your right forefinger squeezes the bottom of the hackle collar up, smashing hackle to either side of the hook.

Smashing hackle collar

Smashed hackle collar

10. Bring the tying thread up behind and cross diagonally forward over the hackle to bring the thread down in front of the far wing. Continue to figure-eight the tying thread until the wings are suitably formed.

Hackle fiber wings formed with thread

11. Figure-eight the wings with very lightly dubbed thread to form a thorax appropriate in size that will also keep the hackle fiber wings in place without distorting their position or shape.

Hackle fiber wings with dubbed thorax.

HAIR TAILS, MOOSE OR ELK

A bundle of eighteen to twenty-four individual moose or elk body hairs roughly equals the diameter of the lead core in a common wood pencil. This is about the right amount to use for tailing a fly on a #12 hook. Use less hair for smaller hooks, more hair for larger ones. Use the amount of hair that looks right to you, but keep in mind the type of water you'll be fishing. Use a little more hair on a fly meant for rough water, to build in some extra flotation. Tie flies for slow-moving streams and lakes a little sparser, to more accurately simulate the naturals.

Black moose body hair is often used on many hair-tailed flies, such as the Royal Wulff and some larger Drakes. As far as I'm concerned, you can use any color of hair on a Royal Wulff, but you would be wise to check out the natural large drakes to see what coloration their tails have. Many are banded dark at the tips, with a light creamy tan band near the center, then become dark again where the tail emerges from the body. If you can find some moose body hair banded like this, hide it from your friends, because it's a perfect match for the tail markings on some flies, and not easy to find.

Elk body hair is a lot easier to get, and nearly any piece of elk hair you pick up will have hair banded in this fashion. Most isn't suitable for tailing, because it's hollow and flares too easily, and the color is too light. However, there is a narrow band of hair on an elk's rump that is nearly perfect for our tailing needs. It's immediately in front of the large blond rump patch that everyone seems to want to get their hands on for dyeing. The hair we want for tailing is a 6- to 8-inch, narrow band of hard (not hollow!) hair that goes up the side of each hip to meet its counterpart at the top of the back. This hair is very straight, and so evens quickly in a hair stacker. It's well banded, plus it's darker than the hair from the rest of the elk's body; and, since it's harder, it doesn't flare when tied to the hook.

1. Tie in the hair tail exactly as described for tying in a hackle fiber tail, except use a little less tension on the first two or three turns of thread, to prevent flaring. Gradually increase the thread tension as you wrap the tailing to the hook shank toward the eye. Stop wrapping forward when you reach a point about a third of the hook-shank length behind the eye. If you want a slim body profile, clip off the tailing butts now. If you want a meatier-looking body, pull the hair butts up and back and lash the butts down on top of the first layer toward the rear of the fly. Clip off the butts at an angle at a point midway between the hook point and the end of the barb. If you are tying a biot-bodied fly, you want a very smooth taper. Biots are slippery and do not stretch. Any bump remaining in the layered tailing butt underbody will cause problems.

NOTE: If you are tying a hair wing (Wulff-style) fly, make sure the clipped butts of the hair wing and the clipped or layered butts of the hair tail form an absolutely smooth junction, especially if you're going to tie a biot-bodied fly.

Single-layer hair tail

Double-layer hair tail

Double-layer hair tail with hair wing

WILD TURKEY BIOTS

Biots are those hard, wide feather fibers on the leading edges of the pointer and primary feathers of a bird's wing. For some reason this versatile natural material has received little attention in fly-tying books. We all use a lot of wild turkey *secondary* wing feathers for winging hoppers, muddlers, and some caddis and stonefly patterns. Duck and goose biots are used frequently in a wide variety of patterns, both in their natural colors and dyed. Once again, I suspect that availability may have a lot to do with this. Now that wild turkeys are becoming more common around the country, good wild turkey secondary wing feathers are readily available. The only use I've heard of for the *pointer* feathers of the wild turkey wing is for fletching arrows.

I discovered turkey biots only because I once ran out of goose biots that were long enough to tie with. When I tried substituting turkey biots, I was amazed at their extra length and at how easy they were to dye. I was also impressed with their strength and pliability; turkey biots aren't nearly as brittle after dyeing as goose biots. All quills and biots should be damp when you tie with them, because they're less likely to break off or be cut by 6/0 or 8/0 thread. Wild turkey biots become very pliable when they're damp. They don't stretch, but they bend easily and—when being wrapped—hold their position over the tailing material much better than goose biots. I pull off the biots one at a time to make a small pile on a wet paper towel folded twice, which keeps them damp while I'm tying.

All you have to do is lift one corner of the folded paper towel to expose the biots you're keeping damp. Not dripping wet, just damp. Be sure they're dry before you store them away after use, or they'll mold. I store unused biots in empty hook boxes, labeled for color on the boxtop.

Folded paper towel with biots

There is a notch on one side of the biot near the base where it was fastened to the quill. If you want the Velcro-like edge of the biot (which is usually dark) to show prominently, tie the biot onto the hook shank so that the notch is toward the eye. This will present a nice ribbed effect, which is desirable on many dun patterns. Be careful, when you take the first turn around the hook shank, that the biot doesn't twist. If that happens, the notch will face the rear of the hook and you won't get the desired effect. Use your hackle pliers on the biot as you would a hackle.

Be careful to build a smooth underbody before attempting to wrap a biot body. Spade hackle tailing will produce a very thin body profile; a single-layer hair tail will present a slightly thicker body; and a double-layer hair tail will yield a more meaty-looking body, such as green and brown drakes have. Study the comparative photos of body profiles below.

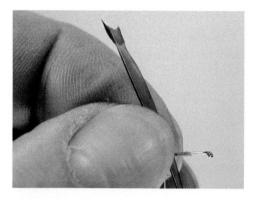

Notch toward hook eye

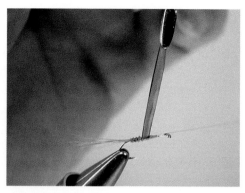

Winding biot body

Completed biot body over hackle fiber tail

Single-layer hair tail and biot body

Double-layer hair tail and biot body

MIDGE WINGS

Finding material for winging midges is a problem for every fly tyer I've ever met. It must be durable, highly visible, very translucent, easy to work with, and available. I have tried few materials that satisfy more than two of these requirements, until recently.

I've found a man-made material (this is a case where I bow to technology) that makes decent midge wings. It's a translucent plastic sheet, impressed with a pattern of thousands of tiny squares that was developed to cover the mandrels upon which sheets of graphite fibers are wrapped to make graphite rods. (A plastic bag manufacturer produces a similar material, but it's too thin for our use.) The graphite rod manufacturers often use scraps of this material for packing filler in those giant tubes they ship rods in. I asked a fly-shop owner to save some for me, and in a couple of weeks he sent me about five pounds of it. When I opened the box I was really upset, because he had jammed the stuff in, just as the rod manufacturers had jammed it into the ends of their shipping tubes. There wasn't one square inch that didn't have a severe crease running through it. It appeared useless. I tried pressing it with a warm iron, and spent the next two hours cleaning melted plastic from our new flatiron. Then I tried it with an old handkerchief between the plastic sheet and the iron. Not only did this remove the wrinkles from the plastic material, it also made it a little shinier on one side, and it became slightly stiffer. Both were major improvements, because the shiner surface reflects more light yet doesn't prevent light from passing through, and the material was a little too soft in the first place. Be careful when ironing this stuff to not allow the iron to remain on one spot; keep the iron set on low-warm, and maintain a constant sweeping motion. Check the progress frequently and stop ironing when the wrinkles have disappeared. Use a steel straightedge and an X-Acto knife to cut the material into strips.

I cut strips ⅛-inch wide for size-18 midges, slightly narrower for size-20, and narrower still for size-22. The width is entirely up to you, though. I use the same material for winging Flying Ant patterns with wider strips for larger hook sizes.

If you keep your eyes open, you'll surely find other sources for material similar to this stuff. For example, as I sit in front of my computer writing this, I notice that the dust cover is made of the same type of material. It's quite a bit heavier and may not work for midge-wing strips, but it's a good example of how it pays to keep your eyes open for anything you might use to fool trout.

1. Wrap the quill body forward into the thorax area two hook-eye lengths behind the eye; tie down and clip off the quill butt on top of the hook shank. Cover the clipped quill butt completely with tying thread to make a very smooth platform for the wing strip.

NOTE: You *must* tie the wing strip on *top* of the body shoulder if you want the wing strip to lie flat on top of the quill body. If you tie on the wing strip in front of the quill body shoulder, the wing will stick up and look more like a mutated mayfly than a midge.

2. Trim the wing strip to an arrow shape, and tie it in by placing it slightly on your side of the hook before you take the first turn of tying thread to anchor it in place; thread torque will move it into position on top of the hook. Keep some tension on the wing strip by pulling toward the rear of the hook as you continue to wrap the point with tying thread.

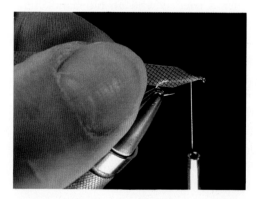

Tying in midge-wing strip

3. The wing strip should come slightly around toward each side of the hook at the tie-down point. This will trap a small bubble of air and aid flotation tremendously. The remainder of the wing strip should flatten over the body of the fly as shown below.

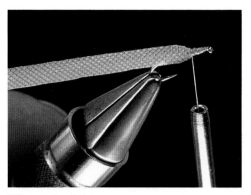

Wing strip tied in

4. Cut off the wing strip at a point where the wing will be about one hook-gap distance longer than the hook. Then trim the corners of the wing as shown in the photo below.

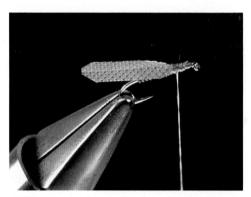

Midge wing trimmed

5. Wrap the hackle so that it covers the wing tie-down area. This usually means tying the butt of the hackle stem onto the hook shank so that the first turn of hackle covers the last wrap of the thread holding down the wing. Be careful to not twist the wing placement as you tie in the hackle. If this happens, you didn't tie in the wing firmly enough. Simply wrap the hackle feather forward toward the eye, tie it off, clip off the excess tip, and whip-finish.

BLACK UGLY NYMPHS

1. Start the tying thread above the hook point, wrap it to the bend, and dub a small ball of dubbing taken from the end of the body wool.

2. Tie in one black-dyed goose biot on each side of the hook directly in front of the ball of dubbing, with the concave side of the biots facing out away from the hook to a length equal to the hook-gap distance.

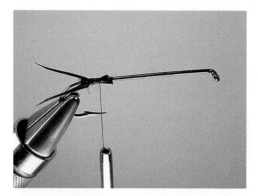

Tail biots tied in

3. Tie in a piece of .030- or .035-inch lead wire on each side of the hook. The front end of the wire should stop about three hook-eye lengths behind the eye; clip off the rear ends directly above the hook point.

Lead wire tied in

4. Cut the end of the 3/32-inch Swannundaze strip at a long angle, then tie it in with the flat side up.

Swannundaze strip trimmed

Swannundaze strip tied in

5. Pull about half the fibers from the end of the body yarn to thin it to about half its original diameter, tie it in by the tip, and twist it a few times to create a tapered rope.

Tapered yarn

Yarn tied in and twisted

6. Wrap the yarn forward to create an evenly tapered body, well into the thorax tie-down area, and clip it off. The thorax area is the front third of the hook.

7. Spiral-wrap the Swannundaze strip forward over the body yarn, tie it down, and clip it off in the same place. Make sure the round side of the Swannundaze is up, or to the outside, as you wrap it forward.

8. Tie in a ¼-inch wide segment of black-dyed goose or wild turkey tail by the butt, shiny-side down and tip pointing over the hook bend. Be certain the quill segment is long enough to reach well past the hook eye when you later pull it forward for the wing case.

9. Tie in the black hen back feather by its tip, shiny-side down, butt pointing over the hook bend. Its individual fibers should be equal in length to the hook-gap distance.

10. Form a dubbing loop, and dub the thorax with dirty orange Australian 'possum (blend orange and tan). Wrap the thorax forward to within two hook-eye lengths behind the eye. Trim the thorax to flatten the top and bottom.

Dubbing thorax   *Trimming thorax*

11. Pull the hen back feather forward, tie it down, and clip it off at the head. Apply a liberal amount of head lacquer along its quill.

12. Pull the quill segment forward, tie it down, and clip it off at the head. Whip-finish, and apply a liberal amount of head lacquer to the head and the wing case.

BLACK UGLY SALMON FLY ADULT

1. Cover the entire hook shank with Danville's Flat Waxed Nylon #100 black tying thread. Bring the tying thread back to the middle of the shank.

ABDOMEN

2. Clip a clump of 2-inch-long black-dyed elk body hair, the diameter of a standard lead pencil; pull out all the underfur, and even the tips, in a hair stacker. Remove the hair and clip the butts so that both tips and butts are exactly even.

Stacked and clipped elk hair bundle

3. Place the clipped butts slightly forward of the middle of the hook (tips to the rear), and tie them down with six or seven very firm wraps of tying thread. Allow the thread torque to distribute the elk hair evenly around the entire hook.

4. Using a medium thread tension, wrap the thread in open spirals around the hair and the hook to the bend, and take six or seven very firm turns of tying thread directly over the bend.

Elk hair tied on and wrapped to bend

5. Pull the flared hair tips forward, and wrap the hair with tying thread in open spirals toward the butts. Create a rear body segment by taking three or four turns of thread in one spot before spiral-wrapping forward. Take six or seven very firm wraps of thread directly over the tied-down butts and clip off the excess hair tips. After the butts have been clipped, wrap the thread toward the rear and then back to the clipped butts, again being careful that the new wraps of thread lie on top of the previous wraps.

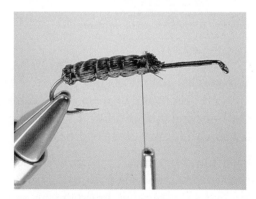

Hair spiral-wrapped to butts

THORAX

6. Clip a clump of 2-inch-long orange-dyed elk body hair equal to the diameter of a standard lead pencil; pull out all the underfur, and even the tips, in a hair stacker. Remove the hair and clip the butts so that the tips and the butts are exactly even.

7. Place the butts four or five hook-eye lengths behind the eye, and tie in the orange hair with six or seven very firm wraps of thread, allowing the thread torque to distribute the hair evenly around the entire shank. Spiral-wrap the thread over the orange hair to the black abdomen, take six or seven very firm wraps of thread, and pull the flared orange tips forward as you did when creating the black abdomen. Be careful to not allow a gap or space to appear between the black abdomen and the orange thorax. Spiral-wrap the thread over the orange tips toward the eye. Clip off the excess orange tips *directly* over the clipped orange butts. Spiral-wrap the thread back to the rear of the thorax.

Completed thorax with thread at center

HACKLE LEGS

8. Tie in two very long and webby black-dyed rooster butt hackles by their tips at the rear of the thorax, and bring the tying thread forward to the front of the thorax. (The hackle fibers should be

at least one-and-one-half times the hook-gap distance.) Take two or three turns of hackle at the tie-down place (to fill in the junction of abdomen and thorax), then open-spiral-wrap the hackles to the clipped front of the thorax.

Hackles tied in

Hackles wrapped

9. Clip the hackle from the top of the fly.

Hackle clipped from top

WING

10. Clip a clump of 2- to 3-inch-long natural gray elk body hair equal in diameter to a standard lead pencil; remove all the underfur and place it in a hair stacker to even the tips. Remove the hair and clip the butts so that the tips and the butts are exactly even.

11. Place the elk on top of the hook with the tips extending one hook-gap distance beyond the end of the bend. Tie down the butts directly over the clipped thorax and anchor with six or seven very firm turns of thread. *Do not allow the thread torque to distribute the hair around the hook.* The wing must remain exactly on top of the hook shank. Spiral-wrap the thread over the wing to the junction of the abdomen and thorax. Try to trap as few hackle fibers as possible, and do not allow thread tension to flare the wing more than twice the diameter of the abdomen. Take four or five turns of thread at the junction, then reverse-wrap the thread back toward the eye. Clip off the excess butts of winging material, and cover them smoothly with tying thread.

Completed wing

12. Select two or three very long and webby black-dyed rooster neck butt hackles, and tie a standard hackle collar. The hackle fibers should be at least twice the hook-gap distance.

GOLDEN STONE NYMPHS

1. Start the tying thread above the hook point, wrap to the bend, and dub a small ball of golden yellow yarn or dubbing.

TAIL

2. Tie in a single biot from a rooster pheasant wing to each side of the hook, with the curved or concave side facing out. The length should equal the hook-gap distance.

3. Lash a piece of .025- or .030-inch lead wire to each side of the hook, with the front ends about three hook-eye lengths behind the eye, and the rear ends clipped off above the point.

SHELLBACK/WING CASE

4. Tie in a ³⁄₁₆-inch side segment of wild turkey secondary wing feather by its tip, shiny-side down, with the clipped butt pointing to the rear. Liberally spray the feather with Krylon Workable Fixatif, to prevent splitting, before separating the segments for tying. Select a feather segment long enough to serve as both shellback and wing case.

Biot tails and shellback tied in

RIBBING

5. Tie in an 8-inch length of Danville's Flat Waxed Nylon #8 yellow directly in front of the shellback tie-down.

BODY

6. Either form a dubbing loop and dub the body with golden yellow dubbing, or tie in a tapered length of golden yellow fine wool yarn. Wrap the abdomen well into the thorax area (the front third of the hook). Tie off the abdomen material, *but do not clip off the excess*; this excess material will be used for the thorax.

7. Pull the shellback segment forward over the body and tie it down with three or four turns of thread. The shellback must be tight from the tail to the tie-down, but be careful to not pull it too hard or you'll tear it off.

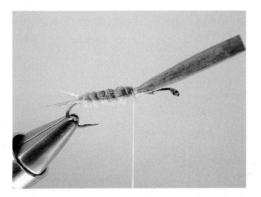

Shellback pulled forward and tied down

8. Wrap the ribbing thread over the body and shellback in an open-spiral-wrap to create the illusion of body segmentation. Be careful to not allow the thread torque to push the shellback to one side of the hook. Fold the shellback segment to the rear and take one or two turns of thread to hold it down. The remaining shellback segment will become the wing case after you've tied in the legs and completed the thorax. Tie off, and clip off the excess ribbing material.

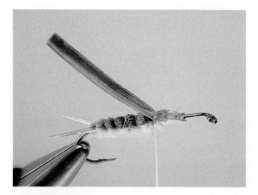

Completed shellback with fold

9. Tie in one mottled light tan hen back feather by its tip, shiny-side down, with the butt of the feather pointing to the rear of the hook. The feather fibers should be equal in length to the hook-gap distance.

Hen back feather tied in

10. Complete the thorax by wrapping a double layer of yarn or dubbing. Tie it down and clip off the thorax material about two hook-eye lengths behind the eye.

11. Pull the hen back feather forward, tie it down, and clip off the excess.

12. Pull the wing case forward over the hen back feather, tie it down, and clip off the excess.

13. Completely cover all clipped materials with tying thread to form a smooth head; whip-finish and lacquer.

GOLDEN STONE ADULTS

1. Cover the entire hook shank with Danville's #8 yellow mono-cord

UNDERBODY

2. Clip a ³⁄₁₆-inch clump of light elk body hair, remove the under-fur, and place the clump in a hair stacker to even the tips. Remove it from the stacker and clip the butts to create a clump of hair with tips and butts that are even at both ends.

3. Place the elk hair on the hook so that the tips extend beyond the beginning of the bend by a distance a little less than half the hook gap, and tie it down firmly beginning at a point about four hook-eye lengths behind the eye. Spiral-wrap to the rear, allowing the thread torque to distribute the hair completely around the hook. Take three or four turns of thread at the beginning of the bend; bring the tying thread back to the tie-down point, and clip off the excess hair butts. Be careful that thread tension does not flare the tips.

Completed elk hair underbody

OVERBODY

4. Tie in the end of the golden yellow yarn over the clipped butts, and spiral-wrap the thread over the yarn and underbody to the rear.

Yarn tied in and thread wrapped to rear

5. Bring the tying thread back to the front tie-down, and carefully wrap the body yarn forward to create a smooth abdomen. Tie it down and clip off the body yarn directly over the clipped under-body hair butts. Trim off as much loose fuzz from the yarn as you can.

Completed body

WING

6. Clip a ³⁄₁₆-inch bundle of natural light elk hair, pull out all the underfur, and place the bundle in a hair stacker to even the tips. Remove the hair and clip the butts to even them. Align the hair on top of the hook shank so that the tips extend beyond the bend by a distance equal to the hook gap. Tie in the butts very firmly

immediately in front of the body tie-down. Using a medium tension on the thread, spiral-wrap the wing to the rear for about a third of the hook shank, then bring the thread forward to the wing tie-down spot. This will create the illusion of a thorax. Do no allow the thread torque to slide the hair around the hook or to flare the wing more than twice the diameter of the body. Clip off the wing butts and cover them smoothly with tying thread.

Completed wing

HACKLE

7. Select two or three medium ginger dry-fly hackles; tie them in and wind a standard hackle collar

LITTLE YELLOW STONEFLIES

1. Completely cover the hook shank with yellow tying thread. Bring the thread back forward and let it hang three hook-eye lengths behind the eye.

BODY

2. Select one 7- to 8-inch stripped yellow-dyed rooster butt hackle quill; clip the tip to a diameter equal to twice that of the hook shank and thread.

3. Tie in the tip of the hackle quill three hook-eye lengths behind the eye, and lash the quill to the top of the shank all the way to the bend. Bring the thread forward to the tip of the quill.

Quill tied in

4. Wrap the quill forward (allowing no spaces between the wraps) to its tip; tie it down on *top* of the hook shank and clip off the excess quill. Completely and smoothly cover the clipped quill butt; the slightest bump in this area will prevent the hen hackle tip wing from seating properly.

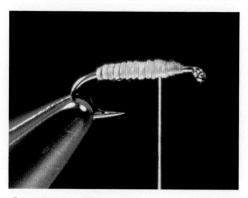

Completed quill body

WING

5. From a neck with feathers that are almost 100 percent web, select one hen hackle feather with a width equal to the hook gap and long enough for its tip to extend beyond the bend by one hook-gap distance. *Do not* clip it to length before tying it in, but do strip away the hackle fibers from both sides of the quill. Gently flatten the quill at what will be the tie-in point with needlenose pliers, and tie it in flat on top of the quill body shoulder with two loose turns of thread. Grasp the butt of the feather with your right hand and pull it forward until you reach the correct wing length. Try to get a few of the hackle fibers to go slightly around either side of the body. Take four or five more turns of thread to anchor the wing firmly in place. Lift the butt and clip it off. Cover the clipped wing butt smoothly with tying thread.

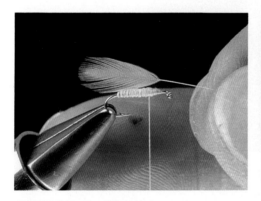

Stripped hen hackle wing

Hen hackle wing tied in

HACKLE

6. Select one pale yellow dyed dry-fly hackle, and wind a sparse hackle collar to cover the front quarter of the hook shank.

CADDIS QUILL LARVAE

1. Completely cover the hook shank with tying thread the same color as the quill you will be using.

2. Select one stripped and dyed 7- to 8-inch rooster neck butt hackle quill, and clip off the tip at a point where the diameter of the quill is equal to twice that of the hook shank and thread.

4. Tie in the clipped tip on top of the shank with the end of the clipped tip about two hook-eye lengths behind the eye. Spiral-wrap the thread over the quill toward the rear of the hook and slightly into the bend. Take several turns of thread and bring the thread back to the initial tie-in point.

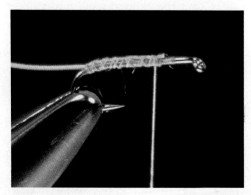

Quill tied in

5. Carefully wrap the quill forward, allowing no spaces between the wraps, to the tie-in point, and tie off the quill on top of the shank. Clip off the excess quill and smoothly cover it with thread.

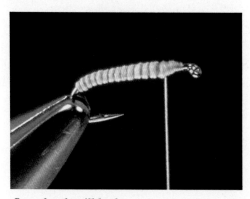

Completed quill body

6. Start black or brown thread behind the eye, wrap it over the light tying thread, and clip off the light thread. Select one long-fibered brown or black ostrich herl; clip off the butt where the fibers are densest, and tie it in by the butt.

7. Wrap the ostrich forward for four or five turns, tie it off, and clip off the excess. Whip-finish, and clip off all the ostrich fibers on the top and sides of the fly.

BLACK AND RED ANTS

1. Dub tiny amounts of fur very tightly onto the thread, and start the rear body segment slightly into the bend of the hook. Wind the dubbing forward in a single layer to directly over the point, and begin winding to the rear again. Repeat until you have built up a teardrop-shaped rear body segment with a diameter equal to about a third of the hook gap. It is very easy to make this portion of the ant body too long. A good rule of thumb when tying the ant pattern is "less is best."

Completed rear body segment

2. Tie in the hackle and wind the hackle collar, leaving a small space between the rear body segment and the first turn of hackle. Four or five turns of hackle is plenty.

Completed hackle collar

3. Dub a tiny amount of dubbing very tightly onto the thread, and
    take only one or two turns for the head.

BLACK AND RED FLYING ANTS

1. Complete steps 1 and 2 above.

2. Clip off all the hackle from the top of the fly, and tie in a strip of
    the same material used for the midge wing. Shape the tie-down
    portion of the strip by clipping it into an arrow shape, then tying
    in the point of the arrow in front of the hackle collar. Clip off the
    strip at a point equal to half the hook-gap distance beyond the
    end of the bend. Round off the corners.

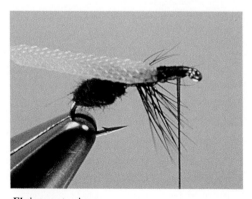

Flying ant wing

3. Head, same as step 3 above.

BEETLES

1. With a steel straightedge and an X-Acto knife, cut the Bugskin into the following widths for corresponding hook sizes:

#14 $\frac{3}{16}$"

#16 $\frac{5}{32}$"

#18 $\frac{1}{8}$"

#20 $\frac{3}{32}$"

#22 $\frac{1}{16}$"

BUGSKIN BEETLE, DUBBED BODY

2. Start the thread immediately behind the eye, and completely cover the shank all the way to the beginning of the bend.

3. Clip one end of the Bugskin strip to an arrowhead shape and very firmly tie in the tip, shiny-side down, at the bend. Carry the tie-down slightly into the bend of the hook.

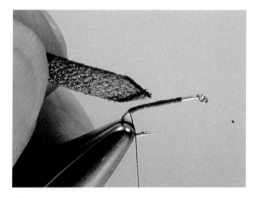

Shaped bugskin

Bugskin tied in

4. Dub a small amount of dubbing onto the thread and create a
    small ball over the Bugskin tie-down. Tie in one hackle feather
    by its tip just in front of the ball, and continue to dub the
    remainder of the body. You want a rather full body profile,   but
    be careful that its diameter doesn't get larger than half the hook-
    gap distance. Stop the body dubbing three hook-eye lengths
    behind the eye.

5. Wind the hackle forward in a closed palmer fashion toward the
    eye. Tie it down and clip off the excess hackle two hook-eye
    lengths behind the eye.

Hackle palmered and tied off

6. Clip all the hackle from the top and bottom of the fly, leaving
    only those hackle fibers that stick out sideways from the body.

Beetle body trimmed

7. Pull the Bugskin strip forward until it is quite firm, and tie it down with five or six very firm wraps of tying thread. Lift the tag end of the strip and carefully clip it off as close to the tie-down as possible. Completely cover the clipped Bugskin with tying thread; whip-finish and lacquer.

BUGSKIN BEETLE, PEACOCK BODY

1. Complete steps 1 through 3 above.

4. Select three or four strong peacock herls; align the butts, and clip off the tips to even the lengths. Tie them in by their tips just over the tie-down of the Bugskin tip. Wrap the peacock herl around the thread several times to reinforce the herl, and take two turns at the rear of the hook to form a small ball of peacock.

Peacock ball tied in

5. Tie in one hackle feather by its tip just in front of the peacock ball, and wrap the herl forward to a point three hook-eye lengths behind the eye. Tie it down and clip off the excess peacock.

6. Wind the hackle forward in a closed palmer style toward the eye. Tie it down and clip off the remaining hackle two hook-eye lengths behind the eye.

7. Repeat steps 6 and 7 above.

A. K.'s HOPPERS (ANY COLOR)

1. Start the thread about one hook-gap distance behind the eye, and firmly cover the hook shank with thread all the way to the bend and back to the starting point.

2. Clip off an 8-inch length of four-strand yarn; tie in the clipped end of the yarn directly over the starting point of the thread, and lash it down all the way to the beginning of the bend. Take several very tight turns of thread at the bend.

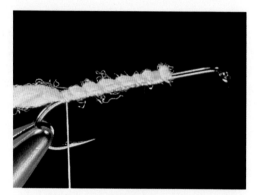

Hopper yarn tied and lashed

3. Twist the remaining yarn to form the extended body loop, and lash it down tightly directly on top of the last wraps of thread holding the wool to the shank.

Extended body loop tied in

4. Tie in the hackle feather by its tip on your side of the hook, immediately in front of the thread wraps that hold the yarn loop in place. The hackle feather should be one size smaller than the hook—i.e., use size-14 hackle for a #12 hook.

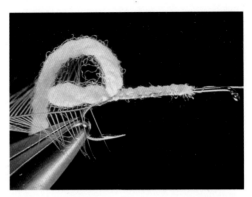

Hackle tip tied in

5. Bring the tying thread forward to the initial yarn tie-in, and firmly wrap the yarn forward to create a smooth body. Tie down the yarn on top of the shank, directly over the initial tie-down. Hold the tag end up and clip it off. Create a smooth, level tying thread platform for the wing tie-down.

Yarn wrapped forward

6. Palmer-wrap the hackle forward and tie it off on *your side* of the hook. Clip off the excess and cover the hackle butt smoothly with tying thread. *Caution: Do not allow the shoulder to become tapered.* See photo.

Completed palmered hackle with square shoulder

7. Clip all the hackle from the top of the body.

8. Saturate a mottle brown wild turkey secondary wing quill with Krylon Workable Fixatif; when completely dry, clip a segment about three-quarters as wide as the hook gap. Fold the segment lengthwise, clip the tip from the center to the edges, then trim the points as shown in the photos below.

Trimming turkey feather segment for wing

9. Place the trimmed and shaped feather on top of the fly's body, and align the clipped tip even with the end of the body loop. Clip off the butt end of the feather segment even with the front edge of the shoulder.

Clipping wing segment to length

10. Apply a liberal drop of head lacquer to the top of the body shoulder, and tie in the wing feather segment with four or five turns of thread, being careful that the segment comes evenly around both sides of the hook. Do not allow the tying thread to slide forward to form a tapered shoulder.

Feather segment with hair wing tied in

11. Tie in a small clump of stacked elk or deer body hair, tips one hook-eye length longer than the feather wing segment. Use only enough thread tension to flare the hair slightly. Pull the hair butts up, but *do not clip them off.*

12. Spin two or three clumps of deer body hair on the *bare* hook shank remaining behind the eye. Tie in the first clump of hair with the butts pointing to the rear. Spin the hair and push it tightly against the shoulder; repeat until you have just enough room left for a whip-finish.

13. Trim the head with a razor blade making the first cut on the bottom of the head, even with the bottom of the turned-down eye. Make successive cuts on either side of the head, keeping the hair

First cut, bottom

Second cut, side

Third cut, opposite side

Fourth cut, top

on the sides about one-and-a-half hook-eye lengths long. Make a fourth cut from front to back on the top of the head. You should have a head that is about a quarter to a third higher in the front than in the rear. Cut off the butts of the winging hair at this time.

NINETEEN

What If Flies

What if I get a chance to fish Ann Marie Lake in Labrador? What if I happen to be near the Henry's Fork some evening in late June or early July? What if I find myself near the Au Sable in Michigan some early July? What if I have a chance to fish the Frying Pan when there's no hatch? What if I want a nymph that looks a little better than the standard issue? What if I need an in-between fly?

I keep dozens of boxes of flies in a side bag with my extra reels and spare spools—all the stuff I don't use regularly. But when I take a fishing trip that's going to last more that two or three days, I can grab that bag and three or four cane rods and know I'm ready for almost any situation. There's even a deck of cards there, in case it rains too hard for me to go fishing—and that's a very hard rain.

Also in this bag are my what if flies. These are flies for special occasions. "Special occasions" usually means fishing for outrageously big fish in a stream or lake that I may never have the opportunity to fish again. I define an "outrageously big fish" as being at least twenty inches long and shaped like a football. An outrageously big fish is one that you would dearly love to have mounted and hanging on the wall of your den but, something inside won't let you kill it. It's a fish so big your friends would think it's a fake! Outrageous fish and the opportunities to go after them are few and far between. That's why I take a little more time tying these what if flies: When I need them, I want them to look better and fish better than any others.

TRICOLOR SHELLBACK NYMPHS

I have been using this nymph pattern for the past fifteen years. I don't carry very many of them, because usually the standard nymph pattern works quite well when I find myself having to fish nymphs. I don't particularly enjoy nymph fishing, but when I do it, I like to catch a few fish. It occurred to me that if tying stonefly nymphs with shellbacks, two-tone segmented bodies, legs, and wing cases was a good idea, perhaps it was just as good an idea to try with mayfly nymphs.

Most mayfly nymph patterns are quite simple: a tail, body, wing case, and clump of throat hackle. That leaves out a lot of detail for a fly presented to the trout at its eye level. All the nymphs I've examined have an abdomen that's lighter on the bottom than on the top or back. The thorax area is usually darker than the bottom of the abdomen, and the top of the abdomen and wing case are darker still. Yet most mayfly nymph patterns use the same color dubbing for all the body and thorax areas. When the stream is crystal clear, there's no hatch, and nothing you

Olive Tricolor Nymph

have tried works, try this nymph pattern in what you think is an appropriate size and color. I tie this pattern from size 20 through size 14 and in two color combinations: light tan to brown, and creamy olive to dark olive.

TRICOLOR SHELLBACK NYMPHS

Hook:	Mustad 3906B or Tiemco 200R, #20-#14.
Thread:	Danville's 6/0 or Uni-Thread 8/0: brown, black or olive.
Tail:	Two or three brown fibers from a rooster pheasant tail feather, or dark brown fibers from a wild turkey tail feather.
Shellback/ *Wing Case:*	Segment of medium dun or dark dun goose wing feather. Spray liberally with Krylon Workable Fixatif before separating into segments.
Ribbing:	Danville's monocord, color darker than abdomen.
Abdomen:	Light tan or light olive rabbit dubbing.
Thorax:	Light brown or dark olive rabbit dubbing. The thorax should be two shades darker than the abdomen.
Wing Case:	Same segment of goose quill.
Hackle:	Dark mottled brown hen back feather segment, tied in as a splayed throat clump.

TYING INSTRUCTIONS:

1. Start the tying thread on the shank directly over the point, and cover the shank to the bend.

2. Tie in two or three tail fibers (check the natural). Take only two or three turns of thread, then push down on top of the tailing fibers with your thumbnail: this should separate them. Place a tiny drop of head lacquer at the tie-down point to hold them in place.

3. Tie in the shellback/wing case by the segment *tip*, shiny-side down, clipped butt pointing away from the eye. Be certain that the feather segment is long enough to serve as a wing case.

4. Tie in an 8-inch length of ribbing.

5. Dub the abdomen, forming a fatter-than-dry-fly taper. Bring the abdomen well into the thorax area.

6. Pull the shellback segment forward on top, and tie it down with two or three turns of thread.

7. Spiral-wrap the ribbing forward, tie it down, and clip off the tag.

8. Fold the wing case back and dub the thorax with darker dubbing, creating a thorax twice the diameter of the abdomen. Don't crowd the eye of the hook, and try to decrease the diameter in a forward taper to prevent the throat hackle from being pushed straight down.

9. Tie in a small clump of soft throat hackle with two or three turns of thread, and press the tie-down with your thumbnail. This should splay the hackle fibers to either side of the hook.

10. Pull the wing case forward and tie it down. Clip off the wing case butt and whip-finish.

11. Apply a liberal amount of head lacquer to the shellback/wing case segment and head.

TRICOLOR SUBEMERGERS

Mayflies are usually treated as nymphs, emergers, adults, and spinners, but I believe there is another point in their cycle that we need to be aware of. The trout seem to think it's important, and so should we. With most mayflies, I define an "emerger" as an insect at that point when the nymph is at the surface and the adult is in the process of crawling out of its wetsuit in preparation for flying away. I define a "subemerger" as one at that point when the nymph is on its way to—but not yet at—the surface; its wing case is beginning to split, and a small portion of the adult wing is beginning to emerge. This fly, which imitates a subemerger, involves a simple addition to the tricolor shellback nymph pattern listed above, and is very effective during the beginning stages of a hatch.

Olive Tricolor Subemerger

TRICOLOR SUBEMERGER

Hook:	Same as Shellback Nymph.
Thread:	Same as Shellback Nymph.
Tail:	Same as Shellback Nymph.
Shellback/ *Wing Case:*	Same as Shellback Nymph.
Ribbing:	Same as Shellback Nymph.
Abdomen:	Same as Shellback Nymph.
Dun Wing Ball:	Light gray yarn segment. Separate four-strand yarn into single strands. Use a single strand for #18 and larger hooks; for #20 and smaller hooks, divide single strands in half. Tie in the tip of the yarn strand on top of the shellback after step 7 above. Double the yarn strand and tie it down again to form a tiny loop. Then complete steps 8 through 11 above.
Thorax:	Same as Shellback Nymph.
Wing Case:	Same as Shellback Nymph.
Hackle:	Same as Shellback Nymph.

FLOATING MICES SHRIMP

There are quite a few freshwater shrimp patterns that have been in the books for many years. They all work, and I've taken a lot of nice trout on just about every shrimp pattern I've tried. But every once in a while something is a little different, and I can't seem to get a trout with anything short of dynamite. Such was the case this fall on the Frying Pan River. Ruedi Reservoir was stocked with mices shrimp some years ago as an additional food source for the lake trout. At certain times of the year, the little crystal-clear shrimp get sucked out and flushed into the Frying Pan, where the trout gorge themselves and grow rapidly into football-shaped monsters.

I spend a week on the Pan once or twice a year and enjoy the outstanding dry-fly fishing. But, as trout fishing sometimes goes, there are days when the bugs decide to take a break. That's when I head upstream to fish the two or three blocks long flats area with a Mices Shrimp in the hope that I might hook a hog. The standard Mices pattern is a very delicate fly, with a sparsely wrapped body of two or three strands of white marabou ribbed with one strand of pearlescent Flashabou. It's white and sparkles. Everything about it looks right. Everyone fishes the pattern with a little lead on the leader above the fly to get it down near the bottom, either fishing it like a nymph with a strike indicator, or casting it across and letting it drift downstream. This day, however, none of the popular tactics worked very well. There were dozens of fish feeding steadily in what appeared to be an emerger rise form. Some fishermen were using BWO emergers, with no luck. The most anyone could hope for was *maybe* one fish an hour. It was exasperating.

I waded out into the stream and watched the water, and made some important discoveries. *All* the shrimps were within an inch or two of the surface. *All* the shrimps were perfectly horizontal to the surface and aligned with the current. *All* the shrimps were so translucent as to be nearly invisible, with tiny black eyes and three or four charcoal-colored markings inside their abdomens. I didn't have a shrimp pattern that looked like these naturals, nor was I fishing the patterns I did have so that they drifted like the naturals. I went back to the truck, opened my fly-tying kit, and looked for something I could use to tie a floating translucent shrimp. The exotic material I found turned out to be a strip of cellophane, which I twisted and wrapped around the hook for the body and thorax. I used five or six white poly yarn fibers for the tail and legs. I quickly tied three on #14 hooks, returned to the stream, found a trout, and caught it.

I changed the presentation by approaching the trout from the side and casting the greased shrimp upstream of the fish. As soon as the fly landed on the water, I tightened the leader to align the fly with the current and keep it at the surface. The first fish weighed 8 pounds in a wet net. I'll claim a 7½-pounder. The next trout was an 18-inch brookie, the third trout a 20-inch brown, the next a 22-inch rainbow, and it continued like that for about an hour. I quit. It was like fishing with bait in a hatchery pond.

It was a great hour or two. I'll do it again, but I won't do it all day or on a daily basis. The real thrill was figuring out the fly and the technique. I've thought a lot about that day during the months since, and I'm wondering if the sudden water-pressure change stunned the shrimps. They got sucked out of the reservoir from a depth of 30 feet or so, and in a matter of seconds found themselves at the surface. They appeared lifeless in the water, but when I netted them and held them in my hand they wiggled feebly. I'm sure there are other reservoirs where this experience might apply.

Floating Mices Shrimp

FLOATING MICES SHRIMP

Hook: Mustad 94840 or Tiemco 100, #16 and #14.

Thread: Danville's 6/0 #1, white.

Underbody: Danville's 6/0 #100 black.

Tail: Five or six fibers of white poly yarn, length to equal hook-gap.

Body: A 6"-long strip of cellophane, cut to taper from a point to a ³/₁₆" width at the butt.

Rear Legs:	Five or six fibers of white poly yarn, extended to hook point.
Eyes:	A ½" length of round black rubber hackle.
Thorax:	Continue with cellophane strip.
Throat Hackle:	Five or six fibers of white poly yarn.

TYING INSTRUCTIONS:

1. Start the white tying thread behind the eye; tie in an 8-inchpiece of black 6/0 thread (underbody), and cover both the black thread and the shank all the way to the bend.

2. Tie in five or six fibers of white poly yarn, length to equal the hook-gap.

3. Tie in the cellophane strip by its point and bring the white tying thread back to the thorax.

4. Spiral-wrap the black thread to the thorax (three or four turns); tie it off and clip off the tag.

5. Hold the butt of the cellophane with hackle pliers and twist until it becomes a round rope from the tie-down to the hackle pliers.

6. Wrap the cellophane rope forward to the rear of the thorax area, being careful to maintain the twists and the rope configuration.

7. Tie in five or six fibers of white poly yarn for the rear legs (length to reach the hook point), using either the cellophane rope or white tying thread.

8. Tie in a ½-inch piece of round black rubber hackle about two hook-eye lengths behind the eye, and figure-eight with thread to hold it across the shank.

9. Continue wrapping cellophane rope to create a thorax about three times the diameter of the abdomen. Tie it off behind the eye, and clip it off.

10. Clip off the rubber hackle flush with the sides of the thorax to form the eyes.

11. Tie in five or six fibers of white poly yarn for the front legs (length to reach rear of thorax), throat-hackle style.

BROWN DRAKES

Many streams famous for daytime hatches also have late-evening-hatching brown drakes. A lot of people are unaware of this, or perhaps they don't care; they may be so tired from casting all day that when dinnertime arrives, they're grateful for the rest. My suggestion is to attempt to contain your enthusiasm until about noon, and then begin fishing the daytime hatches. Then, when everyone else is leaving the stream for dinner, you'll not only have a lot more of the stream to yourself, but you'll also be fresh enough to fish the brown drake hatch when it begins to come off at dusk.

The one or two hours spent fishing the brown drake often result in your biggest fish of the week. Apparently the really big fish can't resist these large drakes hatching in rather quiet water. The nymphs are burrowers and live in the silty bottom areas of the stream. Wading is usually easier since there is less current flow, and although the drakes don't seem to hatch by the thousands, there are usually enough to interest the trout.

The brown drake is a large mayfly best imitated by tying either an extended-body fly on a #12 or #10 standard dry-fly hook, or on a #12 fine-wire 3X-long hook, such as those used for hopper imitations.

Brown drake (photo by John Gierach)

Brown Drake Dun

BROWN DRAKE DUN

Hook:	Mustad 94831 or Tiemco 5212, #10.
Thread:	Danville's monocord #429 tan.
Tail:	Small clump of dark elk hip hair, single layer, length to extend one and a half times the hook gap.
Rib:	Uni-Floss 1X brown.
Body:	Light tan to blond dry-fly dubbing.
Wing:	Light medium dun hen hackle points.
Hackle:	Ginger and grizzly hackle mix.

TYING INSTRUCTIONS:

There are no special techniques for tying this large dry fly. Dub a meaty-looking body and use lots of hackle. I suggest that you clip the hackle from the bottom of the hackle collar even with the hook point. This will help the fly stay upright after it lands on the water, as well as allow it to float heavily on the water, as the natural seems to do.

You may also wish to tie a parachute version of this fly. Use the same recipe as above, except substitute a ½-inch segment of white turkey T-base feather for the wing post. When darkness sets in and the fish are still rising, it's nice to have a fly you can see; this large parachute serves well.

HEXAGENIAS

Some people call any large mayfly a hexagenia, or a brown drake, or even a green drake. When you phone to find out about the hatch and the person on the other end says, "Hexagenias," ask him the following: "What size hook? Is that a long-shank hook? How long is the entire natural in inches, including the tail?" (Usually he won't know, but neither will you if you don't ask.) "What color are the natural's body, wings, and legs?" The answer to the last two questions often yields the most important information. By the mid-1980s, most people knew the difference between a hexagenia and a brown drake, but you'd be wise to ask a few questions before you tie a couple dozen flies and travel a thousand miles to fish for eight-pound trout, only to find you have the wrong fly. Murphy-proof your life.

Chasing the hex hatch can be as spooky as chasing the salmon fly hatch. So many times I arrive before the hatch begins, or I'm a few days late and the hatch is nearly over. Hitting the peak of the hex hatch, though, is one of the most glorious experiences in all of fly fishing. It's easy to forget the little details that contributed to your memory of such a grand evening. You can certainly remember the big fish or the bat that you caught on a backcast, but do you remember the air and water temperatures? The mosquitoes? Did the fly float as you wanted it to? Was a whipporwill nearby? See any raccoons? Was it a humid night? Were there any clouds? There is a lot more to fishing than just catching fish. If you train yourself to remember more of the details, you will learn more about nature *and* improve your chances of hitting the hatch on a more regular basis. A fish diary is valuable less for recording how many fish you caught than for recording all the other little details surrounding the event. It will help remove some of the guesswork from your planning.

The hexagenia is an enormous mayfly, best imitated on a #6 2X-long hook. However, I have found it a little difficult to tie a fly on all that wire that floats well. I don't want to have to change flies every fifteen minutes when it's dark. I want a fly I know will float all evening, even after catching a few fish. The following is a pattern I developed that floats well, presents an acceptable silhouette to the trout, and has some degree of visibility.

Hexagenia

HEXAGENIA

Hook:	Mustad 94831 #8.
Thread:	Danville's monocord #47 brown.
Tail/Extended Body:	Blond elk rump hair.
Wings:	Pair of clear blond hen pheasant breast feathers, or bleached grizzly hen neck or back.
Hackle:	Two or three ginger hackles.

TYING INSTRUCTIONS:

1. Start the thread behind the eye and completely cover the shank all the way to the bend. Bring the thread back to a spot five hook-eye lengths behind the eye.

2. Select a clump of blond elk rump hair at least two inches long. The clump should be about $1/8$ inch in diameter when tied on. Stack the tips and clip the butts to even them. The prepared hair clump should be no less than $1\frac{1}{2}$ inches long.

3. Place the clipped butts on the hook and tie them down very firmly at the shoulder, which should remain five hook-eye lengths behind the eye. The hair tips should extend beyond the end of the bend by $3/4$ inch.

4. Stroke the elk hair to the rear and wrap the tying thread in open $1/8$ inch spirals over and around the hair to the bend. Be sure that the thread torque distributes the hair completely around the shank. Take three turns of thread at the bend and continue spiral-wrapping the thread around the extended hair body for a distance of one hook gap. Take four turns of thread at this point, and reverse-spiral-wrap back toward the shoulder. Take five or six very firm thread wraps at the shoulder tie-down, and clip off the butts. Cover the clipped butts completely with tying thread.

5. Place a tiny drop of Super Glue at the tail end of the thread wraps and clip out the center hairs, leaving four or five hairs on either side for the tail fibers.

6. Select a matched pair of clear blond hen pheasant breast feath-

ers, or bleached grizzly hen neck or back feathers. I like to use hen pheasant because I have a lot of it, and I like the way these feathers maintain their shape even after being greased with flotant. The feather width should be twice the hook-gap distance, and the *completed* wing length should equal the length of the entire hook. Tie in the wings as described for hen hackle wings on page 161, *but* allow an extra hook-eye space behind the wings for a third of the hackle collar.

7. Tie in two or three ginger dry-fly hackles at the same time, and wrap them one at a time to create a full hackle collar. Clip the bottom of the hackle collar even with the hook point.

The spinner is often the most important phase of the hexagenia hatch, and you will need some spinners as well. Use the pattern recipe and tying instructions above, except tie the wings spent, as spinner wings.

CLUMSY DUNS

I came upon this pattern by accident one day several years ago when a friend and I decided to fish the Colorado River in its upper reaches. The stretch near Kremling and Hot Sulphur Springs, Colorado, is known for its good-sized populations of large rainbows and browns, it was the time of year for good blue-winged olive hatches, and we wanted to say we'd done it. It's about a three-hour drive from Boulder, and what we didn't know was that it had begun to rain heavily upstream from our destination about the time we left. By the time we got there, of course, the rain had stopped.

As we approached the stream we could see it was littered with debris and so muddy that if you dropped a dime in two inches of water, you'd be out 10 cents. But the hatch was on—BWOs from bank to bank. But not a single rise. We watched in amazement as the hatch of a lifetime floated by.

We decided to get some bug photos before heading back, and while netting the little size-18 BWOs I noticed that six or seven out of ten insects that floated by had fallen over, and each was struggling to free a wing trapped in the surface film. These insects weren't "stuck in the shuck" or "cripples," they had simply fallen over. There wasn't the slightest breeze and it wasn't raining, so they hadn't been blown over or knocked down by rain. "They must just be clumsy," I thought, and wondered why I'd never seen this before. Suddenly it occurred to me that the trout always get them first! Trout are predators, and like all predators will always take the easy prey. Obviously, we were seeing so many clumsy duns on the water simply because the trout couldn't see them through the muddy water.

Several weeks later, I was fishing the Frying Pan during a good hatch of BWOs and not having much luck, even though I had matched the naturals perfectly with a size-18 Olive Quill Dun. I tried floating nymphs, emergers, parachutes, and spinners, all with little success. Then I remembered the clumsy duns I had seen on the Colorado River. Just for the hell of it I twisted the wings and hackle collar of my fly 45 degrees to the right, to get one wing to lie flat on the water. Then I clipped all the hackle off the bottom of the fly, to get it to lie as flat on the water as possible. It worked like a charm. I didn't catch every rising trout I saw, but my catch rate went up so dramatically that I decided I would never again be without some Clumsy Duns.

I now tie a few Clumsy Duns for all the mayfly patterns I carry, especially for the large drakes. If I run out of Clumsy Duns, I simply give a standard fly a 45-degree twist. It's not exactly a fly of last resort, but it will often save the day for you. When you're catching fish and your partner isn't, and he asks, "What're you using?" you can give an honest answer. Just leave out the part about clumsy.

Clumsy Dun

CLUMSY DUN (twist method)

Very firmly grasp the hackle collar and wings of any mayfly dun pattern with your thumbnail and forefinger, and twist to the right so that the hackle collar, wings, and head all twist as one unit. Hopefully, the tyer was right-handed. If you tie left-handed, give the fly a twist to the left. If you twist the fly in the wrong direction, you'll loosen the thread wraps and the fly could easily come apart. Remember, the grip must be very firm, or you'll tear the hackle collar and wings from the hook.

TYING INSTRUCTIONS:

Tie the fly exactly as you would any mayfly imitation, except tie in the wings at right angles to the hook bend. This is easy to do with a semi-rotary or full-rotary vise. If your vise doesn't rotate, simply give the wings a twist before you completely anchor them to the hook shank before hackling.

Index